The Original
Summer Bridge Activities™

Bridging Grades First to Second

Caution: Exercise activities may require adult supervision. Before beginning any exercise activity, consult a physician. Written parental permission is suggested for those using this book in group situations. Children should always warm up prior to beginning any exercise activity and should stop immediately if they feel any discomfort during exercise.

Caution: Before beginning any food activity, ask parents' permission and inquire about the child's food allergies and religious or other food restrictions.

Caution: Nature activities may require adult supervision. Before beginning any nature activity, ask parents' permission and inquire about the child's plant and animal allergies. Remind the child not to touch plants or animals during the activity without adult supervision.

The authors and publisher are not responsible or liable for any injury that may result from performing the exercises or activities in this book.

Credits

Series Creator: Michele D. Van Leeuwen

Content Editor: Jennifer Stith

Copy Editor: Beatrice Allen

Layout and Cover Design: Chasity Rice

Cover Illustration: Robbie Short

Printed in the USA • All rights reserved.

ISBN 978-1-60418-825-7

About Summer Learning

Dear Parents:

Did you know that many children experience learning loss when they do not engage in educational activities during the summer? This means that some of what they have spent time learning over the preceding school year evaporates during the summer months. However, summer learning loss is something that you can help prevent. Below are a few suggestions for fun and engaging activities that can help children maintain and grow their academic skills during the summer.

- Read with your child every day. Visit your local library together and select books on subjects that interest your child.

- Ask your child's teacher to recommend books for summer reading.

- Explore parks, nature preserves, museums, and cultural centers.

- Consider every day as a day full of teachable moments. Measuring ingredients for recipes and reviewing maps before a car trip are ways to learn or reinforce skills.

- Each day, set goals for your child to accomplish. For example, complete five math problems or read one section or chapter in a book.

- Encourage your child to complete the activities in books such as Summer Bridge Activities™ to help bridge the summer learning gap.

To learn more about summer learning loss and summer learning programs, visit *www.summerlearning.org.*

Have a memorable summer!

Ron Fairchild

CEO, National Summer Learning Association

Table of Contents

About Summer Bridge Activities™

Summer Bridge Activities™: Bridging Grades First to Second prepares your rising second grader for a successful school year. The activities in this book are designed to review the skills that your child mastered in first grade, preview the skills that he or she will learn in second grade, and help prevent summer learning loss. No matter how wonderful your child's classroom experiences are, your involvement outside of the classroom is crucial to his or her academic success. Together with *Summer Bridge Activities™: Bridging Grades First to Second*, you can fill the summer months with learning experiences that will deepen and enrich your child's knowledge and prepare your child for the upcoming school year.

Summer Bridge Activities™ is the original workbook series developed to help parents support their children academically during the summer months. While many other summer workbook series are available, Summer Bridge Activities™ continues to be the series that teachers recommend most.

The three sections in this workbook correspond to the three months of traditional summer vacation. Each section begins with a goal-setting activity, a word list, and information for parents about the fitness and character development activities located throughout the section.

To achieve maximum results, your child should complete two activity pages each day. Activities cover a range of subjects, including phonics, reading comprehension, addition and subtraction, handwriting, character development, fitness, and much more. These age-appropriate activities are presented in a fun and creative way to challenge and engage your child. Each activity page is numbered by day, and each day includes a space for your child to place a colorful, motivational sticker after he or she completes the day's activities.

Bonus extension activities that encourage outdoor learning, science experiments, and social studies exercises are located at the end of each section. Complete these activities with your child throughout each month as time allows.

An answer key located at the end of the book allows you to check your child's work. The included flash cards help reinforce basic skills, and a certificate of completion will help you and your child celebrate his or her summer learning success!

Skills Matrix

DAY	Addition	Fitness & Character Education	Geometry & Measurement	Graphing	Handwriting	Language Arts & Grammar	Number Relationships	Numbers & Counting	Patterning	Phonics	Place Value	Problem Solving	Reading Comprehension	Science	Social Studies	Spelling	Subtraction	Time & Money	Vocabulary	Writing
1					★			★		★										
2	★				★					★			★				★			
3										★			★					★		
4					★	★			★	★										
5										★			★					★		
6		★								★	★								★	
7						★				★		★								
8																		★	★	★
9			★			★							★					★		
10	★									★			★			★	★			
11	★												★				★		★	
12	★					★				★							★			
13			★							★										
14	★					★				★			★				★			
15		★								★		★								
16									★	★			★							
17			★						★	★										
18										★	★		★							★
19		★					★						★						★	
20			★							★			★					★		
BONUS PAGES!														★	★					
1						★											★			
2					★	★	★			★			★							
3	★	★								★		★					★			
4			★									★				★				
5				★						★			★							★
6	★	★														★	★			
7			★							★			★						★	
8										★			★						★	
9						★						★				★				★
10	★							★		★									★	
11										★							★		★	★

Skills Matrix

DAY	Addition	Fitness & Character Education	Geometry & Measurement	Graphing	Handwriting	Language Arts & Grammar	Number Relationships	Numbers & Counting	Patterning	Phonics	Place Value	Problem Solving	Reading Comprehension	Science	Social Studies	Spelling	Subtraction	Time & Money	Vocabulary	Writing
12		★											★				★		★	
13						★					★					★		★		
14						★				★										★
15	★									★			★				★			
16						★											★		★	
17	★	★														★			★	
18	★					★				★						★	★			
19						★				★			★					★		
20	★												★				★		★	★
BONUS PAGES!														★	★					
1	★									★						★	★			
2			★							★						★	★			
3	★									★	★								★	
4						★							★						★	
5										★	★		★							★
6								★					★							
7	★					★							★						★	
8		★	★							★	★									
9					★	★				★		★								
10	★																★	★		★
11											★		★						★	
12	★									★		★	★							
13													★							★
14		★							★								★			★
15	★					★					★									
16						★						★	★							
17	★	★				★							★							
18													★				★			
19													★				★		★	
20				★		★	★													
BONUS PAGES!														★	★					

vii

Encouraging Summer Reading

Literacy is the single most important skill that your child needs to be successful in school. The following list includes ideas of ways that you can help your child discover the great adventures of reading!

- Establish a time for reading each day. Ask your child about what he or she is reading. Try to relate the material to an event that is happening this summer or to another book or story.

- Let your child see you reading for enjoyment. Talk about the great things that you discover when you read.

- Create a summer reading list. Choose books from the reading list (pages ix–x) or head to the library and explore the shelves. A general rule for selecting books at the appropriate reading level is to choose a page and ask your child to read it aloud. If he or she does not know more than five words on the page, the book may be too difficult.

- Read newspaper and magazine articles, recipes, menus, maps, and street signs on a daily basis to show your child the importance of reading.

- Find books that relate to your child's experiences. For example, if you are going camping, find a book about camping. This will help your child develop new interests.

- Visit the library each week. Let your child choose his or her own books, but do not hesitate to ask your librarian for suggestions. Often, librarians can recommend books based on what your child enjoyed in the past.

- Make up stories. This is especially fun to do in the car, on camping trips, or while waiting at the airport. Encourage your child to tell a story with a beginning, a middle, and an end. Or, have your child start a story and let other family members build on it.

- Encourage your child to join a summer reading club at the library or a local bookstore. Your child may enjoy talking to other children about the books that he or she has read.

Summer Reading List

The summer reading list includes fiction and nonfiction titles. Experts recommend that parents read with first- and second-grade children for at least 15 minutes each day. Then, ask questions about the story to reinforce comprehension.

Decide on an amount of daily reading time for each month. You may want to write the time on each Monthly Goals page at the beginning of each section.

Fiction

Cannon, Janell
Stellaluna

Cooney, Barbara
Miss Rumphius

Cummings, Pat
Clean Your Room, Harvey Moon!

dePaola, Tomie
Jamie O'Rourke and the Big Potato
Strega Nona

Eastman, P. D.
Are You My Mother?

Fox, Mem
Wilfrid Gordon McDonald Partridge

Gannett, Ruth Stiles
My Father's Dragon

Hesse, Karen
Come On, Rain!

Hoban, Russell
A Bargain for Frances

Hoffman, Mary
Amazing Grace

Hoose, Phillip M.
Hey, Little Ant

James, Simon
The Birdwatchers
Dear Mr. Blueberry

Kellogg, Steven
Best Friends

Krudop, Walter Lyon
Something Is Growing

Lakin, Patricia
Dad and Me in the Morning

Locker, Thomas
Where the River Begins

Matsuno, Masako
A Pair of Red Clogs

McCloskey, Robert
Blueberries for Sal
Lentil

McLerran, Alice
Roxaboxen

Munsch, Robert
The Paper Bag Princess

Summer Reading List (continued)

Fiction (continued)

Newman, Marjorie
Mole and the Baby Bird

Nolan, Dennis
Dinosaur Dream

Palatini, Margie
Stinky Smelly Feet: A Love Story

Rylant, Cynthia
When I Was Young in the Mountains

Say, Allen
Emma's Rug

Sendak, Maurice
*Pierre: A Cautionary Tale in Five Chapters
    and a Prologue*

Seuss, Dr.
Horton Hatches the Egg
How the Grinch Stole Christmas!

Steig, William
Doctor De Soto
Sylvester and the Magic Pebble

Stevens, Janet
Tops & Bottoms

Stevenson, James
The Castaway

Talley, Carol
Papa Piccolo

Titus, Eve
Anatole

Zagwÿn, Deborah Turney
Apple Batter

Nonfiction

Branley, Franklyn M.
The Big Dipper
Gravity Is a Mystery
What Makes Day and Night

DK Publishing
Eye Wonder: Bugs
Eye Wonder: Reptiles

Gove, Doris
My Mother Talks to Trees

Heiligman, Deborah
Jump into Science: Honeybees

McGovern, Ann
. . . If You Sailed on the Mayflower in 1620

Murawski, Darlyne A.
Bug Faces

Pfeffer, Wendy
Wiggling Worms at Work

Showers, Paul
Where Does the Garbage Go?

Zoehfeld, Kathleen Weidner
*What Is the World Made Of?: All About
Solids, Liquids, and Gases*

Monthly Goals

A *goal* is something that you want to accomplish. Sometimes, reaching a goal can be hard work!

Think of three goals to set for yourself this month. For example, you may want to learn five new vocabulary words each week. Have an adult help you write your goals on the lines.

Place a sticker next to each goal that you complete. Feel proud that you have met your goals!

1. _____ PLACE STICKER HERE

2. _____ PLACE STICKER HERE

3. _____ PLACE STICKER HERE

Word List

The following words are used in this section. They are good words for you to know. Read each word aloud with an adult. When you see a word from this list on a page, circle it with your favorite color of crayon.

amount	opposite
complete	pattern
correct	rhyme
events	sentence
length	solve

Introduction to Flexibility

This section includes fitness and character development activities that focus on flexibility. These activities are designed to get your child moving and to get her thinking about building her physical fitness and her character.

Physical Flexibility

Flexibility to the average person means being able to accomplish everyday physical tasks easily, like bending to tie a shoe. These everyday tasks can be difficult for people whose muscles and joints have not been used and stretched regularly.

Proper stretching allows muscles and joints to move through their full range of motion, which is key to maintaining good flexibility. There are many ways that your child stretches every day without realizing it. She may reach for a dropped pencil or a box of cereal on the top shelf. Point out these examples to your child and explain why good flexibility is important to her health and growth. Challenge her to improve her flexibility consciously. Encourage her to set a stretching goal for the summer, such as practicing daily until she can touch her toes.

Flexibility of Character

While it is important to have a flexible body, it is also important to be mentally flexible. Share with your child that being mentally flexible means being open minded. Talk about how disappointing it can be when things do not go her way and explain how that is a normal reaction. Give a recent example of when unforeseen circumstances ruined her plans, such as having a trip to the park canceled because of rain. Explain that there will be situations in life when unforeseen things happen. Often, it is how a person reacts to those circumstances that affects the outcome. By using relatable examples, you can arm your child with tools to be flexible, such as having realistic expectations, brainstorming solutions to make a disappointing situation better, and looking for good things that may have resulted from the initial disappointment.

Mental flexibility can take many forms. For example, respecting the differences of other children, sharing, and taking turns are ways that your child can practice flexibility. Encourage your child to be flexible and praise her when you see her exhibiting this important character trait.

Draw a line to match each bird with its correct place in line.

1.

third	first	second	fifth	fourth

Say the name of each picture. Circle the letter of each beginning sound.

2.

b   **g**

3.

l   **n**

4.

b   **l**

Say the name of each picture. Circle the letter of each ending sound.

5.

p   **r**

6.

t   **h**

7.

j   **r**

DAY 1

Write the capital letters of the alphabet.

A B

Say the name of each picture. Write the vowel that completes each word.

8.

m____p

9.

c____t

10.

b____d

11.

c____p

12.

p____n

13.

t____p

> **FACTOID:** The largest type of frog is the goliath frog. It can reach up to 12 inches (about 30 cm) in length.

PLACE STICKER HERE

Solve each problem.

1. 5 − 1	2. 6 − 4	3. 3 − 2	4. 3 + 5	5. 9 − 3	6. 8 + 2

7. 3 + 3	8. 7 − 1	9. 8 − 4	10. 2 + 6	11. 7 − 4	12. 3 + 4

Say the name of each picture. Circle the letter of each beginning sound.

13.

v   n

14.

b   x

15.

f   n

Say the name of each picture. Circle the letter of each ending sound.

16.

n   t

17.

m   g

18.

k   y

DAY 2

Write the lowercase letters of the alphabet.

a b

Read each sentence. Draw a picture of your favorite sentence.

19. The cat sat on Alfonso's lap.

The cat plays with the ball.

The boy has a pet frog.

The frog hops on Sam's bed.

The man sat on his hat.

FITNESS FLASH: Touch your toes 10 times.

* See page ii.

PLACE STICKER HERE

Write the correct time for each clock that has hands. Draw hands on each clock that has a time below it.

1.

9:00

2.

4:00

3.

___:___

4.

8:00

5.

___:___

6.

11:00

Say the name of each picture. Write the letter of each long vowel sound.

7.

___

8.

___

9.

___

10.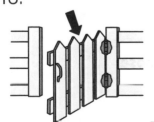

___

11.

___

12.

___

DAY 3

Match each sentence to the correct picture. Write the letter of the sentence in the box.

13. A. Mrs. Wilson pays Henry and Parker for raking the leaves.

B. The ice-cream truck is coming.

C. Parker buys two ice-cream cones.

D. Henry and Parker eat ice cream.

Circle the word that names each picture.

14. tap   tape

15. mop   mope

16. slid   slide

FACTOID: Glass takes one million years to decompose. It can be recycled over and over without wearing out!

PLACE STICKER HERE

Complete each number pattern.

1. 1, 2, _____ , _____ , 5, 6, _____ , _____ , 9, 10, _____ , _____ , 13,

    14, _____ , _____ , 17, 18, _____ , _____ , 21, 22, _____ ,

2. 31, _____ , _____ , 34, _____ , _____ , 37, _____ , _____ , 40, _____ ,

    _____ , 43, _____ , _____ , 46, _____ , _____ , 49, _____

3. _____ , _____ , 77, 78, _____ , _____ , _____ , 82, _____ , _____ , 85,

    _____ , _____ , _____ , 89, _____ , _____ , 92, _____ , _____ , 95,

    _____ , _____ , 98, _____ , _____ , _____

Circle the word that names each picture.

4.	5. 	6. 
can cane	pan pane	pin pine
7. 	8. 	9. 
cub cube	kit kite	cap cape

DAY 4

Practice writing your first and last names.

Write the correct punctuation mark at the end of each sentence. Use (.), (!), or (?).

10. Do you like carrots_____

11. Are bears fuzzy_____

12. Jan can blow bubbles_____

13. Babies drink milk_____

14. Can you jump rope_____

15. Are clouds white_____

16. That movie was great_____

17. Watch out for that puddle_____

18. The woman is happy_____

19. What is your name_____

FITNESS FLASH: Do arm circles for 30 seconds.

* See page ii.

PLACE STICKER HERE

Count the money. Write each amount.

1¢	penny 1¢
5¢	nickel 5¢
10¢	dime 10¢
25¢	quarter 25¢

1. 1¢ 1¢ 1¢ 1¢ _____ ¢

2. 10¢ 10¢ 1¢ 1¢ _____ ¢

3. 10¢ 10¢ 5¢ 1¢ _____ ¢

4. 10¢ 5¢ 5¢ 5¢ _____ ¢

5. 25¢ 25¢ 10¢ 1¢ _____ ¢

Say the name of each picture. Write the letter of each short vowel sound.

6.  ____

7.  ____

8. ____

9.  ____

10.  ____

11. ____

DAY 5

Circle the words that rhyme with the first word in each row.

12.	cat	hat	wig	bat	man	sat
13.	bag	rag	tag	dog	big	sag
14.	he	she	me	we	go	see
15.	cake	rake	late	lake	make	bake
16.	sing	ring	song	thing	wing	big
17.	run	fun	gum	sun	spun	tin

Follow the directions. Color the picture.

18. Draw a tree.

Draw a bird in the tree.

Draw a flower.

Draw a girl sitting on a rock.

Write a title for the picture.

_____

CHARACTER CHECK: Think of a family member who needs your help today. Help her accomplish a task, and you will both feel great.

PLACE STICKER HERE

Count the tens and ones. Write each number.

1. 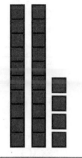 _____

2.  _____

3. 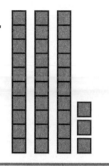 _____

4. 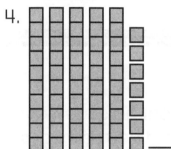 _____

5. 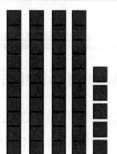 _____

6. _____

Say the name of each picture. Write the letter of each long vowel sound.

7.  _____

8. 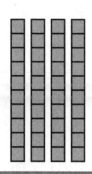 _____

9. _____

10.  _____

11. _____

12.  _____

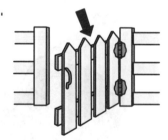

DAY 6

Draw a line to match each word to its opposite.

13.	in	down
14.	up	out
15.	big	short
16.	tall	little

17.	soft	on
18.	hot	cold
19.	off	hard
20.	happy	sad

Move Like a Starfish

Moving around makes you more flexible. Many ocean animals such as crabs, octopuses, and starfish move in unique ways. Practice their ways of getting around. Think about a starfish. It moves by using suction on the bottom of each arm. Pretend that you are a starfish by laying on your stomach, spreading your hands and feet on the floor, and looking facedown. Push up on your toes and hands. Pretend that each of your hands and feet is a starfish foot. Move one "foot" at a time and try to move forward. It requires flexibility to keep your body stretched out. Depending on how far you move like a starfish, you can build strength and endurance too.

FACTOID: Crocodiles are always growing new teeth to replace teeth they lose.

* See page ii.

PLACE STICKER HERE

Solve each problem.

1. Grayson's train has 2 green cars and 7 red cars. How many train cars does Grayson's train have in all?

2. Six deer are standing in a field. Two deer run away. How many deer are left in the field?

3. David has 9 spelling words. He misspells 2 words. How many words does he spell correctly?

4. Magdalena has 7 markers. She finds 3 more markers under her bed. How many markers does Magdalena have in all?

Write a contraction from the word bank that means the same thing as each word pair.

| we'll | it's | you'll | I'm | she'll | they've |

5. it is _____

6. they have _____

7. we will _____

8. I am _____

9. you will _____

10. she will _____

DAY 7

Write each group of words in alphabetical order.

11. apple _____

    cat _____

    book _____

12. dog _____

    fish _____

    eagle _____

13. girl _____

    ice _____

    hat _____

14. lamp _____

    king _____

    map _____

Circle the word that names each picture.

15.

    boy

    bone

    bow

16.

    eagle

    egg

    eye

17.

    sun

    sand

    snake

FITNESS FLASH: Do 10 shoulder shrugs.

* See page ii.

PLACE STICKER HERE

DAY 8

Count the money. Write each amount.

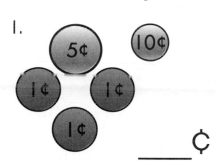

1.

____ ¢

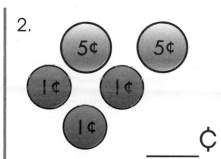

2.

____ ¢

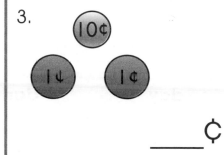

3.

____ ¢

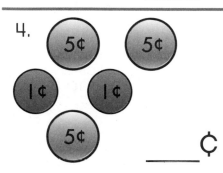

4.

____ ¢

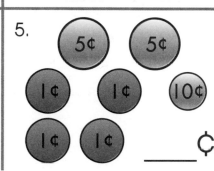

5.

____ ¢

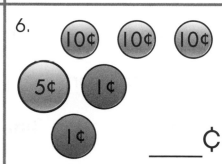

6.

____ ¢

Think of three ways to finish this sentence. Write your sentences on the lines.

I liked first grade because . . .

7. _____

_____ .

8. _____

_____ .

9. _____

_____ .

DAY 8

Circle the word that completes each sentence. Write the word on the line.

10. At night, the sky is _____ .

　　　day　　　　　　**dark**　　　　　　**down**

11. The _____ came to the party.

　　　game　　　　　　**sun**　　　　　　**girls**

12. A rabbit can _____ to the fence.

　　　hop　　　　　　**hat**　　　　　　**boy**

13. Andy's dog got _____ in the pond.

　　　wet　　　　　　**when**　　　　　　**hop**

Fill in each blank. Ask an adult if you need help.

When I was a baby, I learned to talk. I learned to talk when I was _____

months old. My first words were _____, _____,

and _____. If babies could talk even more, they would tell

us _____

_____ .

FACTOID: A person consumes one-tenth of a calorie every time he licks a stamp.

© Carson-Dellosa

PLACE STICKER HERE

Draw a line to match the price of each toy with the correct amount of money.

1. 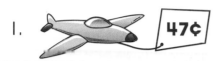 **47¢**

2.  **26¢**

3.  **38¢**

4.  **18¢**

Measure each object with the ruler shown. Write each object's length in inches.

5. 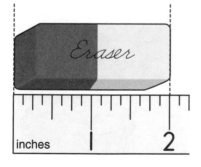 _____ in.

6. 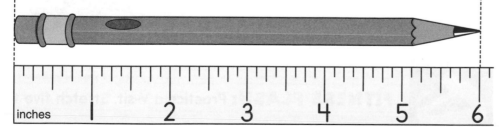 _____ in.

DAY 9

Circle the letter of the phrase that tells what each poem is about.

7. This is a man who is usually wealthy.

    He might live a long time if he keeps himself healthy.

    His castle's his home, but there's one special thing.

    He can always say, "Dad," when he talks to the king.

    A. a king   B. a president

    C. a doctor   D. a prince

8. I've never seen them, but I've heard them scurry.

    When I open the cupboard door, they leave in a hurry.

    They never say please when they take all of our cheese,

    And they don't like our big, gray cat Murray.

    A. relatives   B. mice

    C. friends   D. cats

Write the correct punctuation mark at the end of each sentence.
Use (.) or (?).

9. Do you like puzzles_____

10. We are going to the beach today_____

11. What time do you go to bed_____

12. Is that frog green_____

 FITNESS FLASH: Practice a V-sit. Stretch five times.

* See page ii.

PLACE STICKER HERE

Solve each problem.

1. 5 + 6 = _____

2. 9 – 5 = _____

3. 7 + 3 = _____

4. 8 – 3 = _____

5. 10 + 1 = _____

6. 10 – 4 = _____

7. 2 + 9 = _____

8. 8 – 2 = _____

9. 7 + 4 = _____

10. 9 – 3 = _____

11. 6 + 5 = _____

12. 3 + 8 = _____

13. 9 + 3 = _____

14. 6 + 4 = _____

15. 6 – 4 = _____

Draw a line to match each sentence with the correct job.

EXAMPLE:

I deliver letters and packages.   farmer

16. I help people get well.   pilot

17. I grow things to eat.   mail carrier

18. I fly alrplanes.   teacher

19. I work in a school.   baker

20. I bake cakes and bread.   doctor

DAY 10

Read each word. Color the space blue if the word has the long *i* sound. Color the space green if the word has the short *i* sound.

bib	fry	tie	light	my	sigh	try	wig
six	bike	sign	pie	guy	by	high	if
fib	gift	pit	dry	bite	miss	fish	lit
chin	sit	hill	time	night	hid	bill	quit
bin	mitt	tin	cry	dime	win	fit	will
pin	fine	lie	sight	why	right	shy	fin
zip	ride	buy	side	hike	kite	nine	did

Underline the misspelled word in each sentence. Spell the word correctly on the line.

21. Ebony backed a cake. _____

22. Libby and I whent to the zoo. _____

23. William has a trane. _____

24. Clean your rom! _____

CHARACTER CHECK: Make a list of things you can do to calm down. Then, next time you are upset, refer to your list for help.

PLACE STICKER HERE

Complete each fact family.

1. Family: 2, 3, 5

2 + 3 = ☐

3 + ☐ = 5

5 − 2 = ☐

☐ − 3 = 2

2. Family: 2, 7, 9

7 + 2 = ☐

☐ + 7 = 9

9 − ☐ = 2

9 − ☐ = 7

3. Family: 3, 5, 8

5 + 3 = ☐

☐ + ☐ = 8

8 − ☐ = ☐

☐ − 3 = ☐

Write the correct color words.

4. A snowflake is _____ .

5. Chocolate is _____ .

6. Plums are _____ .

7. Blueberries are _____ .

8. A frog is _____ .

9. A pumpkin is _____ .

10. A banana is _____ .

11. A tire is _____ .

12. Cherries are _____ .

13. A pencil eraser is _____ .

DAY 11

Read the story. Answer the questions.

At the Pond

One warm, spring day, some ducklings decided to go to a pond. They wanted to swim.

"Can we go too?" asked the chicks.

"Chicks can't swim," laughed the ducklings.

"We will run in the tall grass and look for bugs. Please let us go with you," begged the chicks. So, the ducklings and the chicks set off for the pond.

The ducklings swam in the pond. They splashed in the water. The chicks ran in the tall grass. They looked for bugs. The ducklings and the chicks had fun.

After a while, the ducklings and the chicks were tired from playing. They missed their mothers. They missed their nests. It was time to go home.

14. Which sentence tells the main idea of the story?
    A. Ducklings have fun swimming.
    B. Chicks and ducklings hatch from eggs.
    C. The ducklings and the chicks had fun at the pond.

15. Number the story events in order.

    _____ The ducklings swam while the chicks ran in the grass.

    _____ The ducklings wanted to go to the pond.

    _____ The ducklings and the chicks were tired. It was time to go home.

> **FACTOID:** Donkeys can see all four of their feet at the same time.

Solve each problem.

1. 10
   − 6

2. 5
   + 7

3. 10
   − 8

4. 9
   + 7

5. 13
   − 9

6. 16
   − 7

7. 6
   + 8

8. 15
   − 9

9. 7
   + 2

10. 8
    − 3

11. 4
    − 2

12. 2
    + 4

13. 9
    + 2

14. 3
    + 2

15. 4
    + 3

Say the name of each picture. Write the letters for the blend in each word. In a blend, like *sl* in *slide*, two consonants make a sound together.

16.

_____ _____

17.

_____ _____

18.

_____ _____

19.

_____ _____

20.

_____ _____

21.

_____ _____

DAY 12

Draw a line to match each contraction to its word pair.

EXAMPLE:

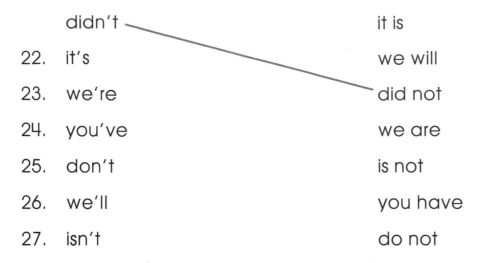

didn't   it is

22. it's   we will

23. we're   did not

24. you've   we are

25. don't   is not

26. we'll   you have

27. isn't   do not

Unscramble each sentence. Write the words in the correct order.

28. swim like Ducks to.

_____

29. we sandbox Can play in the?

_____

30. nests birds in trees Some make.

_____

31. fun today Are having you?

_____

FITNESS FLASH: Do 10 shoulder shrugs.

* See page ii.

PLACE STICKER HERE

Measure each object with the ruler shown. Write each object's length in centimeters.

1.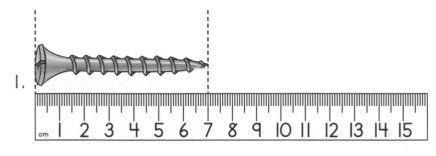

_____ cm

2.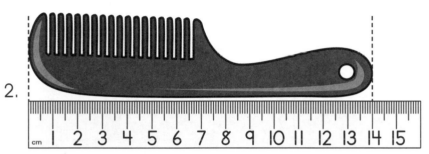

_____ cm

Say the name of each picture. Circle the pictures that have the long _a_ sound, as in _tape_.

cake

hand

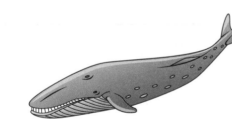

whale

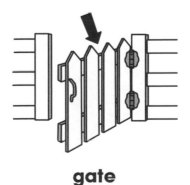

gate

grapes

lamp

Each word and picture make a compound word. Write each compound word on the line.

3. cook +  = _____

4. base + = _____

5. butter + = _____

6. + fighter = _____

Read the word on each balloon. Color the balloon red if the word has the long *u* sound. Color the balloon blue if the word has the short *u* sound.

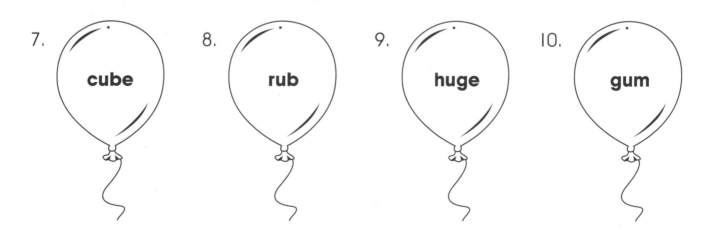

7. cube

8. rub

9. huge

10. gum

FACTOID: A sneeze can travel out of a person's mouth and nose at more than 100 miles (160 km) per hour.

PLACE STICKER HERE

Complete each fact family.

1. Family: 4, 9, 5

    4 + 5 = ☐

    5 + 4 = ☐

    9 − 5 = ☐

    9 − 4 = ☐

2. Family: 6, 2, 8

    6 + ☐ = 8

    2 + ☐ = ☐

    8 − ☐ = 2

    8 − ☐ = ☐

3. Family: 3, 7, 10

    ☐ + ☐ = ☐

    ☐ + ☐ = ☐

    ☐ − ☐ = ☐

    ☐ − ☐ = ☐

Say the name of each picture. Write the letters of the beginning and ending sounds.

4.

____e____

5.
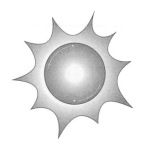
____u____

6.

____a____

7.

____e____

8.

____i____

9.

____a____

DAY 14

Circle the letter of the sentence that describes each picture.

10. A. Dez walked up the stairs.

    B. Dez walked down the stairs.

    C. Dez sat on the stairs.

11. A. Justin threw the baseball to his dad.

    B. Justin threw the baseball to Jessica.

    C. Justin threw the baseball to his mom.

The underlined words tell *who*, *what*, *when*, or *where*. Write the correct word at the beginning of each sentence.

EXAMPLE:

<u>   **who**   </u>   <u>My mother</u> is going home.

12. _____   We will go swimming <u>tomorrow morning</u>.

13. _____   <u>Devon</u> likes to eat peaches.

14. _____   The book is <u>under the bed</u>.

15. _____   On Sunday, we will go on a <u>picnic</u>.

16. _____   The big truck was stuck <u>in the mud</u>.

FITNESS FLASH: Do arm circles for 30 seconds.

* See page ii.

30

PLACE STICKER HERE

Solve each problem.

1. Iman has 3 baseballs. He finds 3 more. How many baseballs does he have in all?

2. A farmer has 9 apples. He makes a pie with 5 of them. How many apples does he have left?

Respect Reminder

What does it mean to respect someone? It means to think about someone else's feelings and to show the person that you care. List the names of the three people whom you respect most and tell why. Then, write how you can show them respect. At the top of your list, write *Respect Really Rules!*

_____

_____

_____

_____

_____

_____

DAY 15

Read the story. Answer the questions.

A Place for Little Frog

Little Frog hopped out of the pond. "Where are you going, Little Frog?" asked the other frogs.

"I am tired of living in this pond with so many frogs," he said. "I need more space." So, Little Frog hopped away.

Soon, he met a bee. When he told the bee his story, the bee buzzed, "You cannot live with me. You would get stuck in my honey."

Little Frog said, "Don't worry, bee, your hive is not the place for me."

Next, Little Frog met a dog. The dog barked and chased Little Frog away. "Living with a dog is not the place for me," said Little Frog.

Little Frog hopped and hopped all of the way back to his pond. The other frogs were happy to see him. They moved over to make room for him. Little Frog settled in, smiled, and said, "Now, this is the place for me."

3. Which sentence tells the main idea of the story?

    A. A hive is no place for a frog.

    B. Dogs do not like frogs.

    C. Little Frog found out that his own home is best.

4. Number the story events in order.

    _____ Little Frog hopped all of the way back to his pond.

    _____ Little Frog hopped out of the pond.

    _____ A dog chased Little Frog away.

CHARACTER CHECK: Share with a friend a time when he showed you kindness.

PLACE STICKER HERE

Draw the next object in each pattern.

1.  _____

2.  _____

3. 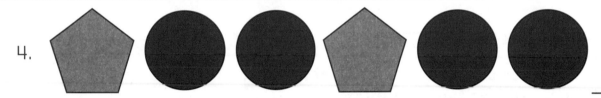 _____

4. _____

Read each riddle. Write a word that rhymes with the underlined word.

5. It rhymes with <u>hat</u>.
It is a good pet.

It is a _____ .

6. It rhymes with <u>boys</u>. Kids like to
play with them.

They are _____ .

DAY 16

Fill in the circle beside the sentence that best describes each picture.

7.

- ○ The bee is on the flower.
- ○ The bee is under the flower.
- ○ The bee is in the hive.

8.

- ○ The bird is on the bowl.
- ○ The bird loves to sing.
- ○ The bird never sings.

Say the name of each picture. Write *1* if the word has one syllable. Write *2* if the word has two syllables.

9.

_____

10.

_____

11.

_____

12.

_____

FACTOID: Although a polar bear appears to be white, its skin is black. Its fur is actually many colorless, hollow tubes.

PLACE
STICKER
HERE

Complete each number pattern.

1. 10, 20, _____ , 40, _____ , _____ , 70, _____ , _____ , 100

2. 5, 10, 15, _____ , _____ , _____ , 35, 40, _____ , _____ , 55, _____ ,

   _____ , 70, _____ , _____ , _____ , 90, _____ , _____

3. 2, 4, _____ , 8, _____ , 12, _____ , _____ , 18, _____ , 22, _____ , 26,

   _____ , _____ , 32, _____ , _____ , _____ , _____ , 42, _____

Say the name of each picture. Write the letter of each vowel sound.

4.  c_____ke	5.  b_____x	6.  d_____ck
7.  l_____mp	8.  m_____lk	9.  m_____ce

DAY 17

**Write the word or phrase that tells where each shape is. The shapes are
on top of, *under*, or *next to* other shapes.**

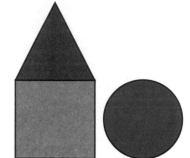

10.   The triangle is _____ the square.

11.   The circle is _____ the square.

12.   The square is _____ the triangle.

**Draw a line to match each butterfly to the flower with the same long
vowel sound.**

great

ā

break

peach

beat

leaf

ē

steak

FITNESS FLASH: Touch your toes 10 times.

* See page ii.

PLACE STICKER HERE

Write how many tens and ones are in each number.
EXAMPLE:

26 = __**2**__ tens __**6**__ ones   1. 41 = _____ tens _____ one

2. 45 = _____ tens _____ ones   3. 84 = _____ tens _____ ones

4. 65 = _____ tens _____ ones   5. 72 = _____ tens _____ ones

6. 17 = _____ ten _____ ones   7. 39 = _____ tens _____ ones

8. 50 = _____ tens _____ ones   9. 51 = _____ tens _____ one

10. 97 = _____ tens _____ ones   11. 100 = _____ tens _____ ones

Draw a line to match each pair of rhyming words.
EXAMPLE:

goat   tree

12. last   band

13. bee   boat

14. sand   fast

15. blue   hair

16. chair   glue

17. mean   rain

18. main   bean

DAY 18

Number the sentences in the order that the events happened.

19. _____ The sun came out. It became a pretty day.

20. _____ It started to rain.

21. _____ Hannah put her umbrella away.

22. _____ Hannah used her umbrella.

23. _____ The clouds came, and the sky was dark.

What do you think the perfect tree house would look like? Describe it and draw a picture of it.

_____

_____

_____

_____

_____

_____

_____

FACTOID: Dust from Africa can travel all the way to Florida.

© Carson-Dellosa

PLACE STICKER HERE

Write > or < to compare each set of numbers.

1. 11 ◯ 13

2. 91 ◯ 87

3. 55 ◯ 75

4. 46 ◯ 29

5. 39 ◯ 27

6. 78 ◯ 33

7. 24 ◯ 19

8. 73 ◯ 85

9. 48 ◯ 100

10. 14 ◯ 21

11. 62 ◯ 56

12. 94 ◯ 78

13. 18 ◯ 47

14. 54 ◯ 62

15. 50 ◯ 44

Color each pair of synonyms the same color.

end

little

small

glad

hear

under

happy

listen

below

finish

DAY 19

Solve each riddle.

16. I am tiny. I have three body parts and six legs. I can be a real pest at picnics. I am an _____ .

17. I was just born. My mom and dad feed me. I cry and sleep, but I cannot walk. I am a _____ .

18. I am made of metal and can be small. I can lock doors and unlock them too. I am a _____ .

19. I have four legs. I like to play. I bark. I am a _____ .

Mount Flex

Become flexible by pretending that you are rock climbing. Lie on your back and stretch your right arm out in front of you as far as you can. Now, stretch your left leg out in front of you toward the sky. Stretch it as far as it will go. Switch arms and legs. Repeat 10 times. Move slowly as you climb the "mountain."

 FITNESS FLASH: Practice a V-sit. Stretch five times.

* See page ii.

PLACE STICKER HERE

Write the correct time for each clock that has hands. Draw hands on each clock that has a time below it.

1.

2:30

2.

___:___

3.

10:30

4.

___:___

5.

5:00

6.

___:___

Say the name of each picture. Circle the letters that make each beginning sound.

7.

ch   wh   sh

8.

ch   wh   sh

9.

ch   wh   sh

DAY 20

Measure each object with the ruler shown. Write the length in inches.

10.

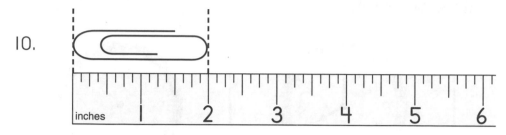

_____ in.

11.

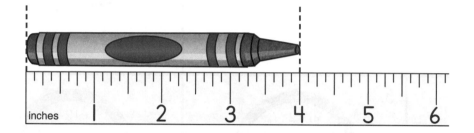

_____ in.

A title tells what a story is about. Write the letter of the title next to the story it matches.

TITLES

A. The Turtle Dream   B. The Sleepover   C. A Wish Before Bed

12. _____ Jenna made a wish every night before going to sleep. She would look in the sky for the brightest star. Then, she would close her eyes and make a wish.

13. _____ Malia fell asleep in the car on the way to the beach. She dreamed that she was a flying turtle. She flew all around the beach. No one could catch her.

14. _____ Kendra had her friend Leslie sleep over. They watched a movie and ate popcorn. They made a tent out of blankets. They slept in the tent.

CHARACTER CHECK: Discuss with an adult what you think is the most important of all good manners.

42

PLACE STICKER HERE

Upside-Down Water

Can you turn a cup of water upside down without spilling it?

Materials:
- index card
- clear plastic cup
- water

Procedure:
1. Do this experiment over a sink.
2. Fill the cup halfway with water.
3. Put the index card on top of the cup. Put your hand over the card. Turn the cup upside down over the sink.
4. Wait two seconds. Then, move your hand away.

What's This All About?

When you flip the cup, the air outside of the cup pushes on the card. The air pushes harder than the water inside the cup. If you wiggle the card before you move your hand, the water molecules on the card and the rim of the cup will stick together. Then, air cannot get in and equalize the pressure.

More Fun Ideas to Try:
- Use different amounts of water in the cup.
- Try different types of paper. You can use construction paper or notebook paper.
- Find out how long you can hold the cup upside down before water starts to spill out.
- Try plastic cups of different sizes and shapes.

BONUS

The Flying Sheet of Paper

How do planes fly?

Materials:

- sheet of paper

Procedure:

1. Hold a sheet of paper just under your bottom lip. Curve the top of the paper slightly. What do you think will happen to the paper if you blow down and across the top of it? Do you think it will hit you in the chest, stay where it is, or bounce up and hit you in the nose?
2. Write your prediction on a separate sheet of paper.
3. Blow down and across the top of the paper.

What's This All About?

By blowing down and across the top of the paper, you cause air molecules to move faster across the paper rather than moving around as they normally do. Faster moving air molecules lower the air pressure on the top of the paper. Higher air pressure under the paper pushes the paper up. For an airplane to fly, the air pressure must be lower on top of the wings than under them. The higher air pressure under the wings pushes the airplane up.

More Fun Ideas to Try:

The next time you take a shower, notice what the shower curtain does. Does it balloon away, or does it move closer to you? Do you know why?

My Own Map

Maps have many uses. A pilot uses maps to find the right flight paths. A hiker uses a map to find her way on a trail. A traveler uses a map to get around a new town.

Work on your mapmaking skills by drawing a map of a path that is in or around your home. You will need a sheet of paper and a pencil. Be as accurate as possible. If you are drawing a path from your room to the refrigerator, include hallways, stairways, rooms, and furniture that you pass as you walk.

Try your map when it is finished. Follow the path as you drew it. Make changes if needed. Then, have a friend or family member try your map. Ask her to use the map to follow the path to the end. Have a surprise treat waiting for her, such as a snack to share.

The State of Things

It is important to learn about where you live. Your state or province might be the home of the first candy factory or the only state or province with a professional trampoline team. With an adult, search the Internet to find interesting information about where you live. Share the fun facts with family and friends. Below are two Web sites to start you on your search.

The Internet Public Library
www.ipl.org/div/stateknow

The World Almanac for Kids
www.worldalmanacforkids.com

International Cuisine

You can learn a lot about other countries by making and eating some of their native dishes. Think of a country you would like to know more about. Find out what foods the people from that country eat. For example, if you want to learn about France, go to the library with an adult and check out French cookbooks or books about French food. Or, search the Internet with an adult to find recipes for French dishes.

Choose a simple recipe with ingredients that you and an adult can buy at your local grocery store. Whether you make soup, salad, or another treat from the country, you will "taste" a bit of the country when you eat the food. Get your family involved. Invite each family member to choose a country and enjoy trying different foods from places around the world.

BONUS

Take It Outside!

In many places, the weather is beautiful outside during the summer. The sun shines. Bright flowers bloom. Color is everywhere. Nature is as pretty as a picture. Make your own art from things that you find outside during the summer. Collect the objects that you discover, such as leaves, stones, shells, flowers, bark, and sticks. Then, make a colorful collage from your treasures.

Grow a plant! All you need is a hand shovel, a seed or seedling, some soil, sunshine, and water. Ask an adult to help you choose what to plant and where to plant it. Whether you plant in a pot or in the ground, it's amazing to give new life to something special. After you plant the seed or seedling, put a paint stirrer or a wooden craft stick in the ground beside it. Then, use a pen to mark the plant's height as it grows taller. Spend the summer watering your plant and watching it grow!

Head outside with a sheet of paper and pencil. Look around and list the things that you see, such as a bush, an ant, a cat, a sidewalk, a bee, a mailbox, a car, and a street. Sort the words into categories. Try to think of at least three ways to sort your words. For example, you could sort the words by their beginning sounds or by whether they name living or nonliving things.

* See page ii.

Monthly Goals

Think of three goals to set for yourself this month. For example, you may want to spend more time reading with your family. Have an adult help you write your goals on the lines.

Place a sticker next to each goal that you complete. Feel proud that you have met your goals!

1. _____

2. _____

3. _____

Word List

The following words are used in this section. They are good words for you to know. Read each word aloud with an adult. When you see a word from this list on a page, circle it with your favorite color of crayon.

adjective	habitat
antonym	homophone
attempts	passage
difference	struggle
fraction	vanish

Introduction to Strength

This section includes fitness and character development activities that focus on strength. These activities are designed to get your child moving and to get him thinking about strengthening his body and his character.

Physical Strength

Like flexibility, strength is an important component of good health. Many children may think that the only people who are strong are the people who can lift an enormous amount of weight. However, strength is more than the ability to pick up heavy dumbbells. Explain that strength is built over time, and point out to your child how much stronger he has become since he was a toddler.

Everyday activities and many fun exercises provide opportunities for children to gain strength. Your child could carry grocery bags to build his arms, ride a bicycle to develop his legs, or swim for a full-body strength workout. Classic exercises such as push-ups and chin-ups are also fantastic strength builders.

Help your child set realistic, achievable goals to improve his strength based on the activities that he enjoys. Over the summer months, offer encouragement and praise as your child gains strength and accomplishes his strength goals.

Strength of Character

As your child is building his physical strength, guide him to work on his inner strength as well. Explain that having strong character means standing up for his values, even if others do not agree with his viewpoint. Explain that it is not always easy to show inner strength. Discuss real-life examples, such as a time that he may have been teased by another child at the playground. How did he use his inner strength to handle the situation?

Remind your child that inner strength can be shown in many ways. For example, your child can show strength by being honest, by standing up for someone who needs his help, and by putting his best efforts into every task. Use your time together over the summer to help your child develop his strength, both physically and emotionally. Look for moments to acknowledge when he has demonstrated strength of character so that he can see the positive growth that he has achieved on the inside.

Count the objects. Solve each problem.

1. Darrell has 3 cookies.
   He eats 2 cookies.
   How many cookies are left?

   $3 - 2 =$ _____

2. There are 6 bananas.
   Pablo eats 3 bananas.
   How many bananas are left?

   $6 - 3 =$ _____

3. There are 7 rabbits.
   Four rabbits hop away.
   How many rabbits are left?

   $7 - 4 =$ _____

4. There are 5 flowers.
   Emma picks 2 flowers.
   How many flowers are left?

   $5 - 2 =$ _____

Write words to describe each object.

5. ice cream

   _____

   _____

   _____

   _____

6. watermelon

   _____

   _____

   _____

   _____

DAY 1

Unscramble each sentence. Write the words in the correct order.

7.   sun shine today will The.

_____

8.   mile today I a walked.

_____

9.   fence We painted our.

_____

10.   me knit will She something for.

_____

Write the words from the word bank in alphabetical order.

| big | little | slow | go | stop | out | up | fast |

11. _____   12. _____

13. _____   14. _____

15. _____   16. _____

17. _____   18. _____

FACTOID: Sloths move so slowly that green algae can grow on their fur.

PLACE
STICKER
HERE

Circle the greater number in each set.

1. 17 or 71

2. 91 or 19

3. 67 or 72

4. 34 or 30

5. 26 or 41

6. 29 or 110

7. 90 or 99

8. 79 or 80

9. 44 or 54

Circle the word that names each picture. Write the word on the line.

10.

glove

glue

11.

frog

flag

12.

clown

clock

13.

bow

bowl

DAY 2

Read each paragraph. Circle the letter of the best title.

14. Carlos is at bat. He hits the ball. He runs to first base and then to second base. Will Carlos make it all of the way to home plate?

    A. Running

    B. Carlos Likes to Play

    C. Carlos's Baseball Game

15. Madison put on sunscreen and sunglasses. Then, she found her favorite green hat. Madison was ready to go outside.

    A. A Rainy Day

    B. Ready to Go Out in the Sun

    C. Madison Likes to Play

Add -s or -es to make each word plural. Write the new words.

16. hand _____

17. kitten _____

18. glass_____

19. inch _____

20. car _____

21. clock _____

22. wish _____

23. brush _____

FITNESS FLASH: Do 10 lunges.

* See page ii.

PLACE STICKER HERE

Solve each problem.

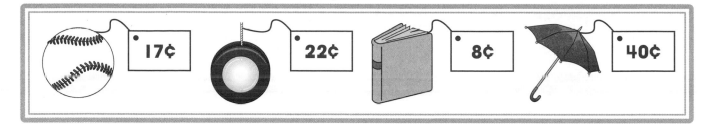

17¢   22¢   8¢   40¢

1. Lori bought an umbrella and a book. How much money did she spend?

2. Henry bought a yo-yo and an umbrella. How much money did he spend?

3. Maria bought a baseball and a yo-yo. How much money did she spend?

4. Alejandro bought a baseball and a book. How much money did he spend?

Leapfrog

Play a fun game of leapfrog to show your strength. Find a friend, sibling, or parent to join you. To play, have one person crouch down low. Have the second person place her hands on the crouching person's back and hop over him. For the first round, pretend that you are frogs. Play more rounds and transform into other hopping creatures, such as grasshoppers, rabbits, and kangaroos. Each time that you hop, remember that you are making your legs stronger and your body healthier! For a bigger strength challenge, invite friends and family members to form a line of crouching critters for you to jump over.

* See page ii.

DAY 3

Add to find each sum.

5. 5
    + 7

6. 8
    + 4

7. 3
    + 7

8. 9
    + 5

9. 15
    + 2

10. 10
    + 6

Subtract to find each difference.

11. 12
    – 8

12. 9
    – 4

13. 11
    – 7

14. 8
    – 8

15. 10
    – 2

16. 6
    – 2

Write the word that matches each set of clues.
EXAMPLE:

It begins like <u>st</u>uck.

It rhymes with <u>late</u>. **state**

17. It begins like <u>r</u>ip.

    It rhymes with <u>cake</u>. _____

18. It begins like <u>t</u>iger.

    It rhymes with <u>bag</u>. _____

19. It begins like <u>c</u>at.

    It rhymes with <u>ball</u>. _____

20. It begins like <u>g</u>um.

    It rhymes with <u>late</u>. _____

FACTOID: A *jiffy* is a real unit of time. It stands for a one-hundredth of a second!

PLACE STICKER HERE

Write how many tens and ones.

1. 46 = _____ tens _____ ones

2. 19 = _____ ten _____ ones

3. 84 = _____ tens _____ ones

4. 64 = _____ tens _____ ones

Write the number.

5. 4 tens and 0 ones = _____

6. 1 ten and 1 one = _____

7. 9 tens and 3 ones = _____

8. 2 tens and 8 ones = _____

Draw the other half of the picture. Color the picture.

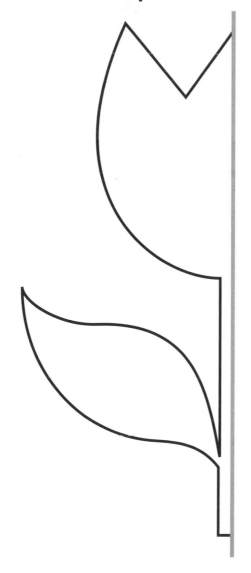

DAY 4

Draw an X on each correct shape in each row.

9.	circle	
10.	parallelogram	
11.	triangle	
12.	trapezoid	
13.	hexagon	
14.	oval	

Underline the misspelled word in each sentence. Then, write each misspelled word correctly on the line.

15. What may I help yu with? _____

16. Please giv him a fork. _____

17. You can sti on the chair. _____

18. Will you miks the paint? _____

FITNESS FLASH: Do five push-ups.

* See page ii.

PLACE STICKER HERE

Which flavor of ice cream is the most popular with your friends and family? Ask each person to choose a favorite ice-cream flavor from the list. Mark a tally beside each answer given.

vanilla _____   banana _____

chocolate _____   cherry _____

strawberry _____   other _____

Count the tally marks beside each flavor. Graph your results.

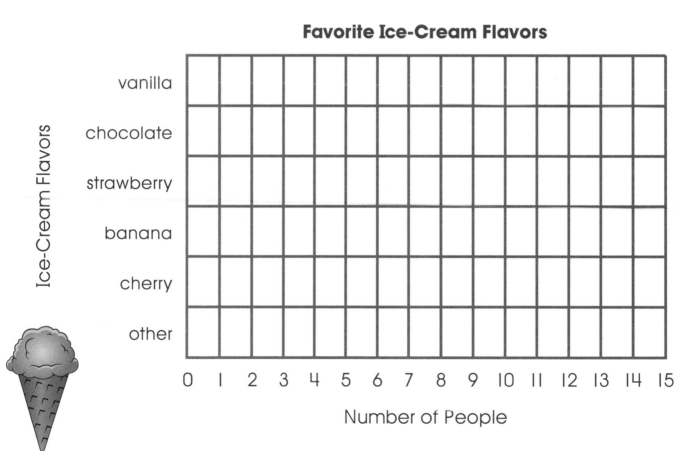

Favorite Ice-Cream Flavors

Ice-Cream Flavors

vanilla, chocolate, strawberry, banana, cherry, other

0 1 2 3 4 5 6 7 8 9 10 11 12 13 14 15

Number of People

Describe the funniest dream you have ever had. Write about it on a separate sheet of paper.

DAY 5

Read the story. Answer the questions.

Olivia lives on a farm. She wakes up early to do chores. Olivia feeds the horses and chickens. She also collects the eggs. Sometimes, she helps her dad milk the cows. Her favorite thing to do in the morning is eat breakfast.

1. Where does Olivia live? _____

2. Why does she wake up early? _____

3. Write one chore that Olivia does. _____

4. What is her favorite thing to do in the morning? _____

_____

Say the name of each picture. Write the vowels to complete each word.

5.

c____ ____n

6.

b____ ____l

7.

____ ____l

CHARACTER CHECK: Form a neighborhood cleanup crew. With an adult and some friends, walk through your neighborhood and pick up litter. Your neighborhood will be a cleaner place!

PLACE STICKER HERE

Add to find each sum.

1.	2	2.	1	3.	4	4.	5	5.	2	6.	4
	2		1		4		5		3		3
	+ 2		+ 1		+ 4		+ 5		+ 2		+ 0

7.	5	8.	3	9.	4	10.	6	11.	7	12.	10
	4		3		6		4		0		10
	+ 5		+ 3		+ 5		+ 2		+ 7		+ 10

Rain Forest Animals

Have you ever seen the way animals of the rain forests move? Some animals, such as monkeys, swing from tree branch to tree branch. Some animals, such as sloths, slowly climb trees by stretching up and down. Read about a rain forest animal. Then, create your own stretch. Try to move like your chosen animal. Share your new stretch with a friend. Can she guess which animal you are?

* See page ii.

DAY 6

Draw a line to match each pair that has the same difference.

13.	5 – 3	5 – 1
	8 – 3	9 – 8
	8 – 4	7 – 2
	5 – 4	6 – 4

14.	8 – 7	10 – 4
	3 – 1	4 – 3
	8 – 2	5 – 3
	9 – 5	7 – 3

15.	10 – 5	13 – 10
	12 – 6	7 – 1
	2 – 0	9 – 4
	9 – 6	4 – 2

16.	5 – 5	14 – 7
	12 – 9	8 – 5
	11 – 4	8 – 8
	12 – 8	5 – 1

Unscramble each word. Spell each word correctly on the line to complete each sentence.

17. Juan had a _____ for _____ mother.
    igft **ihs**

18. The _____ has a _____ tire.
    acr **tfla**

19. A butterfly _____ on _____ flower.
    ats **hte**

20. My _____ works at the _____ .
    add **tsoer**

FACTOID: You'll never see elephants playing hopscotch. Why? Because they can't jump!

PLACE STICKER HERE

Read each paragraph. Underline the sentence that states the main idea.

1. Sidney's umbrella is old. It has holes in it. The color is faded. It doesn't keep the rain off of her.

2. Tabby is a farm cat. He is tan and white. Tabby helps the farmer by catching mice in the barn. He sleeps on soft hay.

3. Big, gray clouds are in the sky. The wind is blowing, and it is getting colder. I think it will snow.

Antonyms are words that have opposite meanings. Write an antonym for each underlined word. Circle each antonym in the word search.

4. The opposite of <u>clean</u> is

    _____.

5. The opposite of <u>night</u> is

    _____.

6. The opposite of <u>hot</u> is

    _____.

7. The opposite of <u>light</u> is

    _____.

8. The opposite of <u>laugh</u> is _____.

v	d	i	r	t	y	e	h	k
a	b	a	m	c	e	u	d	g
x	c	r	y	o	d	s	a	j
w	l	h	o	l	r	j	y	n
q	a	z	c	d	d	o	w	n
d	a	r	k	b	s	s	l	m
h	r	e	p	s	t	d	j	p

DAY 7

Will the figures stack flat on top of each other? Circle *yes* or *no*.

9.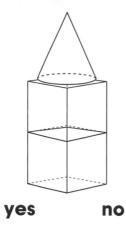

yes   **no**

10.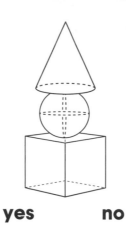

yes   **no**

11.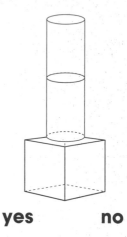

yes   **no**

Read each word. Write *e* if the *y* makes the long *e* sound, as in *story*.
Write *i* if the *y* makes the long *i* sound, as in *sky*.

12. ☐ baby   ☐ fly   ☐ windy   ☐ bunny   ☐ fry

13. ☐ shy   ☐ family   ☐ buy   ☐ happy   ☐ jelly

14. ☐ cry   ☐ my   ☐ funny   ☐ silly   ☐ try

FITNESS FLASH: Do 10 squats.

* See page ii.

PLACE STICKER HERE

Circle the word in each row that does not belong.

I.	bean	carrot	book	lettuce	peas
2.	train	jet	leg	car	boat
3.	cat	orange	green	blue	red
4.	lake	ocean	pond	chair	river
5.	bear	apple	lion	wolf	tiger
6.	Jane	Kathy	Tom	Jill	Anna
7.	park	scared	happy	sad	mad
8.	tulip	daffodil	rose	daisy	basket

Write *oi* or *oy* to complete each word. Write the word on the line.

9. **b**_____ _____

_____

10. **t**_____ _____

_____

11. **s**_____ _____**l**

_____

12. **p**_____ _____**nt**

_____

13. _____ _____**ster**

_____

14. **v**_____ _____**ce**

_____

Read the story. Answer the questions.

Flying High

Ethan is a baby bald eagle. He is learning to fly. It has been a real **struggle** for Ethan. He has been practicing for days, but he does not seem to be improving.

Getting up in the air is easy. Flying over fields is no problem. But, Ethan has trouble flying around things. He does not do well when he **attempts** to land on a certain spot. Perhaps he should sign up for flying lessons to improve his flying skills.

15. The word **struggle** means:

   A. something that is not easy

   B. a boat

   C. a broken wing

16. In the story, the word *he* stands for:

   A. Ethan's friend

   B. Ethan

   C. the teacher

17. The word **attempts** means:

   A. sings

   B. tries

   C. waits

FACTOID: If a cranberry is ripe, it will bounce. Cranberries are also called bounceberries!

PLACE STICKER HERE

Write the correct verb to complete each sentence.

1. Amelia _____ a song.

   sing   sang

2. Did the bell _____ yet?

   ring   rang

3. The grass_____ green.

   is   are

4. She _____ a race.

   run   ran

5. Mom will_____ a short trip.

   took   take

6. Chris _____ a new scooter.

   has   have

If you could plant a garden, what would you plant and why?

_____

_____

_____

_____

_____

_____

DAY 9

Solve each problem.

7. Cara spent 18¢. Danielle spent 10¢. How much did they spend altogether?

8. Pilar has 10 stamps. Edward has 15 stamps. How many stamps do they have altogether?

9. Nelan has 16 fish. Jay has 12 fish. How many fish do they have in all?

10. Emily has 13 balloons. Jessi has 10 balloons. How many balloons do they have in all?

Unscramble each word. Spell each word correctly on the line. Use the word bank to help you.

crop	most	frog	sled	glad	stone	land	swim

11. grof _____

12. nald _____

13. etsno _____

14. lgda _____

15. stom _____

16. prco _____

17. miws _____

18. desl _____

FITNESS FLASH: Do 10 sit-ups.

* See page ii.

PLACE STICKER HERE

Add to find each sum. Draw a line to match each dog with the correct bone.

1. 32
    + 21

2. 73
    + 24

3. 20
    + 10

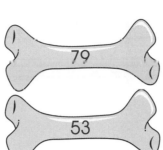
79

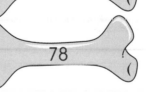
53

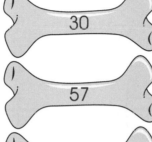
30

57

97

78

4. 44
    + 13

5. 52
    + 26

6. 61
    + 18

Say the name of each picture. Circle the letters that make each ending sound.

7.

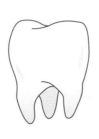

th   sh   ch

8.

th   sh   ch

9.

th   sh   ch

DAY 10

Complete each number line.

Count by 2s.

10.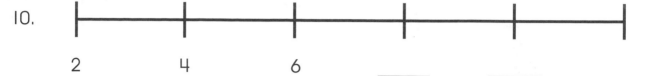

2   4   6   ____   ____   ____

Count by 4s.

11.

4   ____   12   ____   ____   ____

Count by 5s.

12.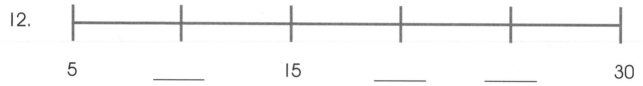

5   ____   15   ____   ____   30

Answer each question using a word from the word bank.

go	no	far

13. Write the word that means the opposite of <u>near</u>. _____

14. Write the word that means the opposite of <u>yes</u>. _____

15. Write the word that means the opposite of <u>stop</u>. _____

CHARACTER CHECK: Talk with an adult about the best time and way to ask for something.

PLACE STICKER HERE

Write the correct homophone for each underlined word. Use the word bank to help you.

bee	eight	hear	knot
right	sea	through	wood

1. Denise <u>ate</u> _____ small pancakes for breakfast.

2. Stay <u>here</u> and you can _____ the music.

3. Can you <u>see</u> the _____ from the top of the hill?

4. <u>Be</u> careful when you catch a _____ !

5. <u>Would</u> you get some _____ for the fire?

6. Did you <u>write</u> the _____ answer?

7. He <u>threw</u> the ball _____ the hoop.

8. The man could <u>not</u> tie a _____ in the rope.

Have you ever helped someone without the person knowing? How did you feel?

_____

_____

_____

_____

DAY II

Rearrange the letters in the phrase *camping trip* to make new words. Write the words on the lines.

camping trip

_____

_____

_____

Draw a line to divide each compound word into two words. Write the words on the line.

9. goldfish
_____

10. popcorn
_____

11. daytime
_____

12. doghouse
_____

13. spaceship
_____

14. railroad
_____

15. blueberry
_____

16. sailboat
_____

17. grapefruit
_____

18. cupcake
_____

19. newspaper
_____

20. sometime
_____

FACTOID: Millions of trees are accidentally planted by squirrels because they forget where they hid the nuts!

Subtract to find each difference.

1. 10
   − 2

2. 10
   − 9

3. 10
   − 7

4. 10
   − 1

5. 10
   − 8

6. 10
   − 6

7. 10
   − 3

8. 11
   − 9

9. 11
   − 7

10. 11
   − 2

11. 11
   − 8

12. 11
   − 4

13. 11
   − 3

14. 12
   − 2

15. 12
   − 9

16. 12
   − 1

17. 12
   − 8

18. 12
   − 7

Synonyms are words that have the same meanings. Antonyms are words that have opposite meanings. Underline the synonym and circle the antonym for the first word in each row.

19.	big	large	little	dog
20.	fast	slow	car	quick
21.	glad	silly	sad	happy
22.	smile	grin	mouth	frown
23.	sunny	bright	cloudy	play

DAY 12

Number the sentences in the order that the events happened.

24. _____ Jenny made a chocolate cake for her friend.

25. _____ Jenny put blue frosting on the cake.

26. _____ Jenny put sprinkles on the cake.

27. _____ Jenny went to the store and bought a box of cake mix.

Draw and color a picture of the cake that Jenny made.

Integrity Issues

Integrity means that you always do the right thing, even when no one is watching. Having integrity is always doing what you feel is right whether you are in front of a group, with one person, or alone. On a separate sheet of paper, write what you would do in the following situation:

You helped start a school recycling program because you know that taking care of the earth is important. You are outside when you finish your granola bar, and you do not see a trash can anywhere. What do you do with the wrapper?

FITNESS FLASH: Do 10 lunges.

* See page ii.

PLACE STICKER HERE

Color the balloon whose number matches each description. Use the color listed.

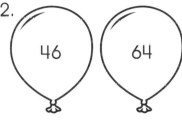

1.

32   23

2 tens and 3 ones
blue

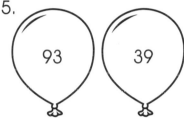

2.

46   64

4 tens and 6 ones
green

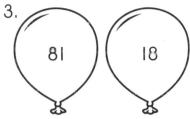

3.

81   18

1 ten and 8 ones
purple

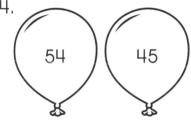

4.

54   45

5 tens and 4 ones
orange

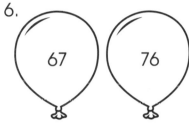

5.

93   39

3 tens and 9 ones
black

6.

67   76

6 tens and 7 ones
brown

In each sentence, one word is misspelled. Write the correctly spelled word from the word bank on the line.

| barn | help | pet | wet |

7. A dog is a good pat.

_____

8. The horse sleeps in the banr.

_____

9. She ran to get hilp.

_____

10. The paper got wit.

_____

DAY 13

Read each sentence. Circle each noun. A noun can be a person, place, or thing.

11.   The boy lost his shoe.

12.   She wrote a letter to her aunt.

13.   Did you have a sandwich?

14.   We saw a movie about butterflies.

15.   My little sister has a brown teddy bear.

Write the months of the year in order.

October	March	February	April
December	July	November	June
August	May	January	September

_____   _____

_____   _____

_____   _____

_____   _____

_____   _____

_____   _____

FACTOID: Some types of bamboo can grow more than 40 in. (100 cm) per day.

PLACE STICKER HERE

Circle the odd numbers in each row.

1. 2   5   7   3   9   4   6   11   14

2. 1   10   6   7   12   13   15   2   17

3. 5   11   9   13   14   17   19   3   8

Circle the even numbers in each row.

4. 6   9   2   11   4   7   3   8   12

5. 13   8   10   6   12   16   9   5   19

6. 14   16   9   11   12   18   7   4   8

Write the missing consonant in each word.

7.	8.	9.
 ca_____el	 se_____en	 ti_____er
10.	11.	12.
 spi_____er	le_____on	 ru_____er

DAY 14

Write the correct word to complete each sentence.

13. A dime is a _____ .
                  coin   coyn

14. I want to buy my friend a new _____ .
                             toi   toy

15. My cat has one white _____ .
                        paw   pau

16. Dan has two sons and one _____ .
                          daughter   dawter

Invent and design a new kind of juice box. Draw your design below. Describe your new juice box on a separate sheet of paper.

FITNESS FLASH: Do 10 squats.

* See page ii.

PLACE STICKER HERE

Read the passage. Answer the questions.

Black-Footed Ferrets

Years ago, many black-footed ferrets lived in the American West. They were wild and free. Their **habitat** was the flat grasslands. This habitat was destroyed by humans.

The ferrets began to **vanish**. Almost all of them died. Scientists worked to save the ferrets' lives. Now, the number of ferrets has increased.

1. Where did the black-footed ferrets live?

   _____

2. Who worked to save the ferrets? _____

   _____

3. What happened after scientists started to help the ferrets?

   _____

4. The word **habitat** means:
   A. a costume worn by ferrets
   B. a pattern of behavior
   C. a place where something lives

5. The word **vanish** means:
   A. to be born
   B. to disappear
   C. to clean one's home

DAY 15

Write the correct numbers to get the answer in each box.

6. 4 – _____ =

    3 + _____ =

    2 + _____ =

    3

7. 5 + _____ =

    2 + _____ =

    9 – _____ =

    6

8. 7 + _____ =

    _____ – 1 =

    _____ – 3 =

    8

9. _____ – 4 =

    8 – _____ =

    3 + _____ =

    5

Write the correct contractions.

10. cannot _____

11. I am _____

12. you are _____

13. do not _____

14. he is _____

15. I will _____

Write the two words in each contraction.

16. didn't _____

17. isn't _____

18. you've _____

19. she's _____

20. couldn't _____

21. we're _____

CHARACTER CHECK: Discuss with an adult what you think are the three most important qualities of a good friend.

PLACE STICKER HERE

Write *is* or *are* to complete each sentence.

1. We _____ going to town tomorrow.

2. This book_____ not mine.

3. Where _____ a box of cereal?

4. Seals _____ fast swimmers.

5. _____ he planning to help?

6. _____ you going to the festival?

Write a sentence using *is*.

_____

Write a sentence using *are*.

_____

Write the correct punctuation mark at the end of each sentence. Use (.), (!), or (?).

7. Are we going to the park_____

8. Look out for the ball_____

9. I know you can do it_____

10. Do bulls have horns on their heads_____

11. The girl on the bike is my sister _____

DAY 16

Subtract to find each difference.

| 12. | 15
– 4 | 13. | 14
– 2 | 14. | 16
– 8 | 15. | 17
– 3 | 16. | 13
– 4 |

| 17. | 10
– 4 | 18. | 18
– 7 | 19. | 13
– 6 | 20. | 11
– 9 | 21. | 16
– 5 |

Find a synonym in the word bank for each word. Write the synonym on the line.

angry	big	close	funny	happy
ill	quick	scared	start	tidy

22. begin _____

23. shut _____

24. sick _____

25. mad _____

26. glad _____

27. neat _____

28. large _____

29. fast _____

30. afraid _____

31. silly _____

FACTOID: Slugs have four noses to help them smell chemicals in water.

PLACE
STICKER
HERE

Circle the scrambled word in each sentence. Spell each word correctly on the line.

1. A brzea is an animal with stripes. _____

2. The robin has nowlf away. _____

3. We mixed flour and oil in a owlb. _____

4. Button your button and zip your rpzipe. _____

5. A lot of leppeo were at the playground. _____

6. We met our new neighbors yatdo. _____

7. My old oessh do not fit. _____

Genuine Jungle Gym

Your favorite playground can become your personal gym! Get on the monkey bars and carry yourself across for a great arm and upper-body workout. Use a park bench to hold your feet while you do sit-ups to increase your core strength. Exercise does not have to feel like work. Just play hard, be creative, and have fun. Think of ways to challenge yourself, and you will build your strength.

* See page ii.

DAY 17

Add to find each sum.

8.	9.	10.	11.	12.	13.
3	6	9	5	4	2
5	4	2	1	3	3
+ 2	+ 3	+ 2	+ 2	+ 4	+ 5

14.	15.	16.	17.	18.	19.
4	7	1	6	2	8
5	2	8	1	3	2
+ 3	+ 1	+ 1	+ 4	+ 2	+ 3

Find a synonym in the word bank for each underlined word. Write the synonym on the line.

automobile	glad	rush	small

20. The ladybug is very <u>tiny</u>. _____

21. The <u>car</u> ran out of gas. _____

22. Casey won, so he was very <u>happy</u>. _____

23. My uncle was in a big <u>hurry</u>. _____

 FITNESS FLASH: Do five push-ups.

* See page ii.

PLACE STICKER HERE

Color each shape to show the fraction.

1.

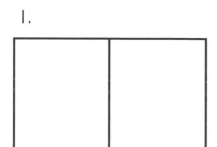

$\dfrac{1}{2}$

2.

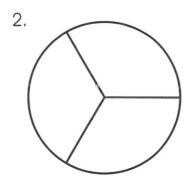

$\dfrac{1}{3}$

3.

$\dfrac{1}{4}$

Draw a line to match each contraction to the word pair that makes the contraction.

 wasn't

 he's

 she'd

 it's

 they'll

 they will

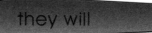 she would

 it is

 he is

 was not

DAY 18

Solve each problem.

4. 71
    + 7

5. 48
    + 1

6. 32
    + 7

7. 53
    − 3

8. 17
    − 2

9. 90
    + 6

10. 23
    + 5

11. 64
    − 3

12. 85
    + 3

13. 72
    + 4

14. 42
    − 1

15. 67
    + 2

Unscramble each word. Spell each word correctly on the line.

16. ribd _____

17. eack _____

18. nebo _____

19. lebl _____

20. gbrni _____

21. ithkn _____

22. oonn _____

23. ppayh _____

24. seay _____

25. dbyo _____

FACTOID: The Sahara desert covers 3.5 million square miles (9 million square km) or about one-third of Africa.

PLACE STICKER HERE

Write the best adjective from the word bank to complete each sentence. An adjective is a word that describes a person, place, or thing.

funny	furry	hard	oak	red	six

1. His kite got caught in that _____ tree.

2. I cannot believe you ate _____ apples.

3. We laughed at the _____ clowns.

4. Kayley got a _____ bike from her parents.

5. My pillow is very _____ and lumpy.

6. The rabbits all have soft and _____ ears.

Circle the main idea of each picture.

7.

A. The boy gives his sister a balloon.

B. The boy is young.

8.

A. The children are wearing masks.

B. The children are standing together.

DAY 19

Circle the coins that add up to the amount shown.

9.

10¢

10.

16¢

11.

25¢

12.

45¢

Draw a line to match each pair of homophones.

13.	ate	one	18.	pair	blue
14.	cent	hour	19.	hear	pear
15.	our	sent	20.	know	write
16.	won	new	21.	right	here
17.	knew	eight	22.	blew	no

FITNESS FLASH: Do 10 sit-ups.

* See page ii.

PLACE
STICKER
HERE

Solve each problem.

1.	10	2.	18	3.	7	4.	7	5.	8
	− 4		− 14		− 3		+ 5		+ 2

6.	6	7.	9	8.	11	9.	11	10.	10
	− 4		− 4		− 1		+ 8		− 8

11. 8 + 6 = _____   12. 9 + 3 = _____   13. 4 + 9 = _____

Draw a line to match each pair of antonyms.

14.	strong	new	21.	always	short
15.	bad	sad	22.	light	fast
16.	over	weak	23.	slow	off
17.	old	good	24.	tall	never
18.	happy	under	25.	on	sink
19.	add	dry	26.	inside	dark
20.	wet	subtract	27.	float	outside

DAY 20

Read each sentence. Follow the directions.

Draw a plate on a place mat.

Draw a napkin on the left side of the plate.

Draw a fork on the napkin.

Draw a knife and spoon on the right side of the plate.

Draw a glass of juice above the knife and spoon.

Draw your favorite lunch on the plate.

Complete the writing activity.

If I could fly anywhere, I would fly to _____ because

_____

_____

_____

_____

CHARACTER CHECK: Gather your outgrown gently-used toys and books and give them to a local shelter.

PLACE STICKER HERE

Super Sediment

What sinks to the bottom of a river first—soil, sand, or pebbles?

Materials:
- 3 paper cups
- sand
- funnel
- soda bottle (2-liter with cap)
- soil
- pebbles
- water

Procedure:
1. Fill one paper cup with soil, one cup with sand, and one cup with pebbles. These will be the sediment.

2. Use the funnel to pour the soil, sand, and pebbles into the bottle. Pour water into the bottle until it is almost full. Close the cap tightly.

3. Shake the bottle until everything is mixed well.

4. Place the bottle on a table. On a separate sheet of paper, draw a picture of what you see in the bottle. Watch as the sediment begins to settle.

5. Check the bottle after 15–30 minutes. Draw what you see.

6. Check the bottle again in 24 hours. Draw what you see.

What's This All About?
Sediment is the soil, sand, and pebbles that wash into streams, rivers, and lakes. In nature, sediment piles up and forms sedimentary rocks.

In the bottle, you have created a small body of water with a lot of sediment. The larger pieces of sediment settle to the bottom more quickly. The smaller pieces of sediment are more likely to float in the water longer and settle to the bottom more slowly.

* See page ii.

Sweet, Sour, Salty, Bitter

Did you know that you can make a taste map of your tongue?

Materials:
- lemon (cut in half)
- pretzel
- water
- grapefruit rind
- sugar cube

Procedure:
1. Touch the inside of a lemon to the very tip of your tongue. Do you taste it? Don't move your tongue around. Rinse your mouth with water. Touch the lemon to the middle of your tongue. Do you taste it? Rinse your mouth with water. Touch the lemon to the sides of your tongue. Do you taste it?

2. Rinse your mouth with water. Repeat the activity with the pretzel, the grapefruit, and finally the sugar cube.

What's This All About?

There are four main tastes that humans can tell apart: sweet, sour, salty, and bitter. Your tongue is divided into different taste zones. Each taste zone is a certain area of your tongue. In this activity, you should discover which parts of your tongue detect each kind of taste.

More Fun Ideas to Try:

Based on your experiment, draw a taste map of your tongue. First, draw a picture of your tongue in the box. Then, label each area where you tasted salty, sweet, sour, and bitter.

* See page ii.

Look What I Did!

A time line is a list of dates that tells important things that have happened. You have already had a lot of things happen in your lifetime. Make a time line to show your accomplishments, milestones, and important events. Ask an adult to help you. If you have a baby book, scrapbooks, photo albums, or other records, use those things to help too. You will need a piece of poster board and markers to create the time line. List at least 10 different events to show a variety of activities. If possible, attach photos or drawings to highlight the events. This is a fun way to look back at your history. Display the time line in a special place in your bedroom. Add to it as you grow and do more.

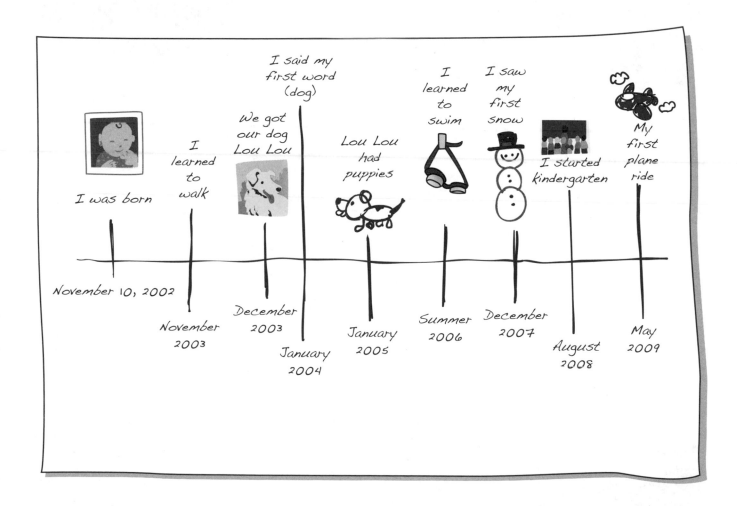

Sandbox Relief Map

Some maps help people find their way. Other maps show physical features (things like oceans and mountains) of places. These are called relief maps. Make your own relief map in a sandbox. Get out your shovel and pail to dig and build. Be sure to make features such as a mountain, a lake, a river, a hill, an ocean, an island, a volcano, a desert, a forest, and a valley. Add water to fill up the water features. Use things that you find in nature, such as rocks, to build the mountains. Find some small sticks for trees and bushes. Soon, you will have your own real-life relief map.

* See page ii.

Having a Ball on Earth

A globe is a 3-D map that shows what the earth looks like. Make your own globe with a beach ball or large plastic ball and markers. Draw a line around the middle of the ball to represent the equator. The equator is a pretend line that marks the middle of the world. Label the top of the ball *north pole* and the bottom of the ball *south pole*. The north and south poles are places that mark the top and the bottom of the earth. Draw and label the seven continents (Africa, Antarctica, Asia, Australia, Europe, North America, and South America) and the four major oceans (Arctic, Atlantic, Indian, and Pacific). Place a star sticker on the globe to represent the place where you live. Toss the globe around with a friend or family member and try to learn the names of the important places that you marked. Soon, you will know more about the earth than you did before.

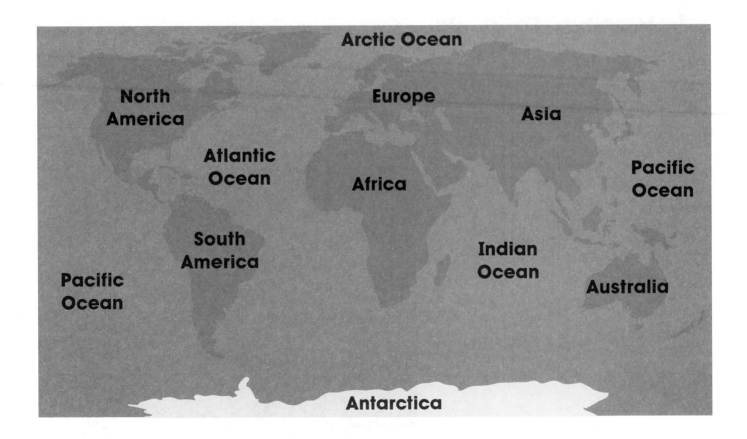

BONUS

Take It Outside!

Set up a safe, mini-obstacle course in a grassy area. Use soft objects, such as piles of cut grass or piles of leaves. Arrange the items in a line. When you reach the end of the course, turn around and retrace your steps to repeat it. Vary the way that you go through the course, such as running, hopping, crabwalking, or skipping.

Take a friend, sibling, or parent outside with you and challenge him to a "rhyme-off." Find a spot to sit down and begin by pointing out an object that you see, such as a rose. Invite your partner to think of a real word that rhymes with *rose*, such as *nose*. (*Zose* will not work.) Go back and forth until neither of you can think of any other rhyming words. Then, pick a new outside word and start again.

Play outdoor opposites. The park is perfect for this game. While you're there, look around. Try to find opposite events that are happening. For example, you might see a sad toddler who fell when playing but a happy dog rolling in the grass. See how many opposites you can find!

* See page ii.

Monthly Goals

Think of three goals to set for yourself this month. For example, you may want to do 30 math problems in one minute. Have an adult help you write your goals on the lines.

Place a sticker next to each goal that you complete. Feel proud that you have met your goals!

1. _____
   PLACE STICKER HERE

2. _____
   PLACE STICKER HERE

3. _____
   PLACE STICKER HERE

Word List

The following words are used in this section. They are good words for you to know. Read each word aloud with an adult. When you see a word from this list on a page, circle it with your favorite color of crayon.

addend	map
cause	opinion
effect	rhythm
energy	subtract
fact	sum

Introduction to Endurance

This section includes fitness and character development activities that focus on endurance. These activities are designed to get your child moving and to get her thinking about developing her physical and mental stamina.

Physical Endurance

Many children seem to have endless energy and can run, jump, and play for hours. But, other children may not have developed that kind of endurance. Improving endurance requires regular aerobic exercise, which causes the heart to beat faster and the person to breathe harder. As a result of regular aerobic activity, the heart becomes stronger, and the blood cells deliver oxygen to the body more efficiently. There are many ways for a child to get an aerobic workout that does not feel like exercise. Jumping rope and playing tag are examples.

Summer provides a variety of opportunities to bolster your child's endurance. If you see your child head for the TV, suggest an activity that will get her moving instead. Explain that while there are times when a relaxing indoor activity is valuable, it is important to take advantage of the warm mornings and sunny days to go outdoors. Reserve the less active times for when it is dark, too hot, or raining. Explain the importance of physical activity and invite her to join you for a walk, a bike ride, or a game of basketball.

Endurance and Character Development

Endurance applies to the mind as well as to the body. Explain to your child that *endurance* means to stick with something. Children can demonstrate mental endurance every day. For example, staying with a task when she might want to quit and keeping at it until it is done are ways that a child can show endurance.

Take advantage of summertime to help your child practice her mental endurance. Look for situations where she might seem frustrated or bored. Perhaps she asked to take swimming lessons, but after a few early-morning classes, she is not having as much fun as she had imagined. Turn this dilemma into a learning opportunity. It is important that children feel some ownership in decision making, so guide her to some key points to consider, such as how she asked all spring for permission to take lessons. Remind her that she has taken only a few lessons, so she might get used to the early-morning practices. Let her know that she has options to make the experience more enjoyable, such as going to bed earlier or sleeping a few extra minutes during the morning ride to lessons. Explain that quitting should be the last resort. Teaching your child at a young age to endure will help her as she continues to develop into a happy, healthy person.

Complete each table.

1.

Add 10	
5	15
8	
7	
9	
3	
4	

2.

Add 8	
2	
6	
4	
7	
3	
5	

3.

Add 6	
10	
6	
8	
7	
4	
5	

Circle the word that is spelled correctly in each row.

4. ca'nt   can'nt   can't
5. esy   easy   eazy
6. kea   key   kee
7. buy   buye   biy
8. liht   light   ligte
9. wonce   onse   once
10. carry   carey   carre
11. you're   yure   yo're
12. star   stor   starr
13. funy   funny   funnie

DAY 1

Use each fact family to write two addition and two subtraction number sentences.

14.

___8___ + ___5___ = ___13___

_____ + _____ = _____

_____ − _____ = _____

_____ − _____ = _____

15.

_____ + _____ = _____

_____ + _____ = _____

_____ − _____ = _____

_____ − _____ = _____

16.

_____ + _____ = _____

_____ + _____ = _____

_____ − _____ = _____

_____ − _____ = _____

Write each word from the word bank under the word that has the same vowel sound.

| coat | drove | fox | job |
| rock | rope | those | top |

nose   **pop**

_____   _____

_____   _____

_____   _____

_____   _____

FACTOID: Did you ever wonder how night butterflies avoid hungry bats? They have ears on their wings!

PLACE STICKER HERE

Complete each table.

1.

Subtract 5	
9	4
5	
7	
10	
11	
8	

2.

Subtract 3	
10	
9	
7	
8	
6	
11	

3.

Subtract 2	
11	
7	
9	
5	
8	
6	

Say the name of each picture. Circle the letters that you hear in the word.

4.

ir   or   er

5.

ur   or   ar

6.

ir   or   ar

7.

or   ur   ar

8.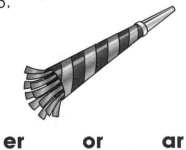

er   or   ar

9.

ir   er   ar

DAY 2

Use the mileage maps to answer the questions.

10. How many miles is it from Salt Lake City to Bountiful? _____

11. How many miles is it from Provo to Pleasant Grove? _____

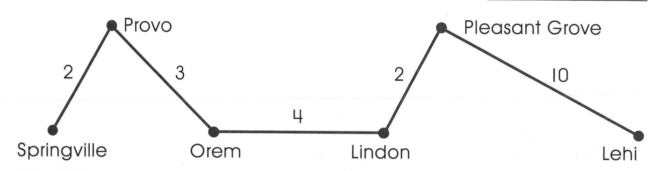

Read each sentence. If the underlined word is spelled correctly, circle _yes_. If the underlined word is not spelled correctly, circle _no_.

12.	Uma is a very <u>brav</u> girl.	yes	no
13.	The United States flag is red, white, and <u>bloo</u>.	yes	no
14.	Those girls were in my <u>class</u>.	yes	no
15.	Gina is a very <u>helpfull</u> friend.	yes	no
16.	I turned off the <u>light</u>.	yes	no
17.	This glue is sticky <u>stuf</u>.	yes	no
18.	Is <u>shee</u> coming with us?	yes	no

 FITNESS FLASH: Do 10 jumping jacks.

* See page ii.

PLACE STICKER HERE

Add to find each sum.

1. 24 + 12	2. 28 + 11	3. 32 + 26	4. 42 + 27	5. 12 + 11
6. 75 + 24	7. 15 + 24	8. 91 + 14	9. 40 + 40	10. 82 + 16
11. 18 20 + 11	12. 41 6 + 32	13. 66 22 + 11	14. 13 22 + 24	15. 30 12 + 10

Circle *g* if the word begins like *game*. Circle *j* if the word begins like *gel*.

16. giant g j	17. giraffe g j	18. goat g j
19. gate g j	20. golf g j	21. gentle g j
22. gym g j	23. gem g j	24. girl g j

DAY 3

Count the hundreds, tens, and ones. Write the number.

25.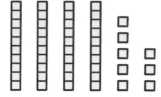

_____ hundreds, _____ tens,

and _____ ones = _____

26.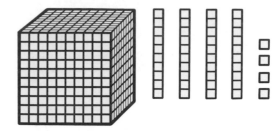

_____ hundred, _____ tens,

and _____ ones = _____

27.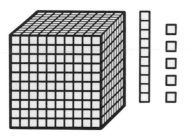

_____ hundred, _____ ten,

and _____ ones = _____

28.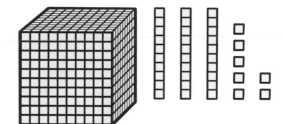

_____ hundred, _____ tens,

and _____ ones = _____

Write one sentence for each meaning of the word _bat_.

29.　bat:　a wooden stick that is used to hit a ball

　　　bat:　a small animal that flies at night

_____

_____

FACTOID: At least 26 rocks from Mars have landed on Earth.

PLACE
STICKER
HERE

Write the numeral for each number word.

1. ninety-six _____   2. twenty-one _____

3. eighty-two _____   4. thirty-seven _____

5. sixty-five _____   6. sixty-one _____

7. seventy-nine _____   8. fifty-eight _____

9. twenty-two _____   10. eighty _____

11. eighteen _____   12. one hundred _____

Draw a line to match each phrase with the word it describes.

13. The time of day when the sun goes down is   A. clock.

14. The place where dolphins live is the   B. bird.

15. Something near you is   C. babies.

16. A crow is a kind of   D. snail.

17. An object that tells time is a   E. close.

18. Apples are a kind of   F. sunset.

19. A small animal with a shell is a   G. ocean.

20. A shop is a kind of   H. first.

21. The winner comes in   I. store.

22. Chicks, ducklings, and fawns are animal   J. fruit.

DAY 4

Read the poem.

My Cat

Have you seen my cat?
Yes, I've seen your cat.

Really? My cat is big.
I saw a big cat.

My cat has spots.
I saw a big cat with spots.

My cat's spots are black.
I saw a big cat with black spots.

My cat runs fast.
I saw a big cat with black spots running fast.

You did see my cat! Where is it?
I don't know. I saw it last week.

Draw a line to connect each word with its antonym.

23. big   black

24. slow   little

25. white   fast

Answer the questions.

26. What is the poem about?_____

27. Describe the cat. _____

_____

FITNESS FLASH: Hop on your left foot 10 times.

* See page ii.

106

PLACE STICKER HERE

Color the shape whose number matches each description.

1.

2 tens and 3 ones

2.

5 tens and 7 ones

3.

5 tens and 2 ones

4.

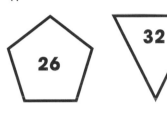

2 tens and 6 ones

5.

3 tens and 9 ones

6.

1 ten and 0 ones

Write each word from the word bank under the word that has the same vowel sound.

blow	bowl	brown	clown	crown
elbow	how	mow	own	tower

cow   **pillow**

_____   _____

_____   _____

_____   _____

_____   _____

DAY 5

Write the letter of each cause beside its effect.

Effects	**Causes**

7. _____ Justin put on his hat and mittens.

A.   It was cold outside.

8. _____ Chloe put ice in the water.

B.   Her feet had grown.

9. _____ Ahmet gave his dog a bath.

C.   The bike's tires were flat.

10. _____ Evan put air in his bike tires.

D.   The rabbit was hungry.

11. _____ Kari got a new pair of shoes.

E.   The water was warm.

12. _____ The rabbit ate the carrot.

F.   The dog played in the mud.

Imagine that you are going on a trip. You can take only one thing. What would you take? Why?

_____

_____

_____

_____

CHARACTER CHECK: Make a list of things you can do to show respect to animals.

PLACE STICKER HERE

Circle the correct rule for each number pattern.

1.

2, 4, 6, 8, 10, 12

+2   +1

2.

20, 18, 16, 14, 12, 10

−2   −3

3.

50, 60, 70, 80, 90, 100

−10   +10

4.

80, 79, 78, 77, 76, 75

+10   −1

Say the name of each picture. Write the letters to complete each word.

5.

so____ ____

6.

____ ____apes

7.

fi____ ____

8.

____ ____irt

9.

____ ____ide

10.

ki____ ____

Read the passage. Answer the questions.

Stamp Collecting

Are you a **philatelist**? If you collect stamps, that is what you are! Stamp collecting is a fun and interesting hobby.

If you want to start collecting stamps, you will need a few supplies. You will need a pair of tweezers to move the stamps so that they do not get dirty. You will also need an album with plastic pages to store your stamps.

Start by collecting some stamps. The stamps you collect can be new or used. You can collect stamps from letters that are delivered to your house. You can also buy stamps to add to your collection.

Next, decide how to sort your stamps. You can group them by their value, by the places they are from, or by the types of pictures on them. Then, place the stamps in your album.

Keep your stamp album in a cool, dry place away from direct sunlight. Heat, sun, and dampness can ruin your stamps.

11. Which sentence tells the main idea of the passage?

    A. Stamp collecting is a fun and interesting hobby.

    B. You can organize stamps in many different ways.

    C. Stamps come from all over the world.

12. What is a **philatelist**? _____

    _____

FACTOID: Some lungfish can survive out of the water for more than two years.

Write a fraction that shows how much of each shape is colored.

1.

$\dfrac{}{}$

2.
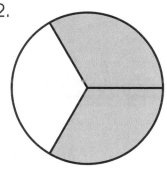

$\dfrac{}{}$

3.
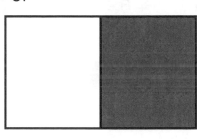

$\dfrac{}{}$

Complete each sentence with the correct compound word from the word bank.

cartwheel	fireworks	grandfather
snowflakes	sunflower	waterfall

4. The _____ lit up the night sky.

5. My mother's dad is my _____ .

6. In gym class, we learned how to do a _____ .

7. The _____ is a large, yellow flower.

8. When the first _____ fall, we know winter is coming.

9. We pitched our tent near a beautiful _____ .

DAY 7

Solve each problem. Circle the largest sum in each row.

10. $6 + 5 =$ _____ $0 + 9 =$ _____ $7 + 8 =$ _____ $8 + 9 =$ _____

11. $8 + 8 =$ _____ $3 + 6 =$ _____ $9 + 9 =$ _____ $5 + 7 =$ _____

12. $6 + 3 =$ _____ $5 + 5 =$ _____ $9 + 4 =$ _____ $7 + 9 =$ _____

13. $8 + 3 =$ _____ $2 + 2 =$ _____ $9 + 5 =$ _____ $6 + 7 =$ _____

Read the story. Circle each answer that makes sense. There may be more than one answer.

14. Murphy's mom quickly pulled everything out of the dryer. Then, she lifted the lid of the washer, looked inside, and shook her head. She looked around the kitchen and family room, and then she rushed upstairs. "I cannot find it," she called to Murphy. "The last time I saw it was after the game on Saturday. We have to find it before 4:00!"

A. Murphy's mom has friends coming over at 4:00.

B. Murphy's mom is looking for Murphy's soccer jersey.

C. Murphy has a game today at 4:00.

D. Murphy's mom lost her purse.

FITNESS FLASH: Hop on your right foot for 30 seconds.

* See page ii.

PLACE STICKER HERE

Use a metric ruler to measure each object. Write the length in centimeters.

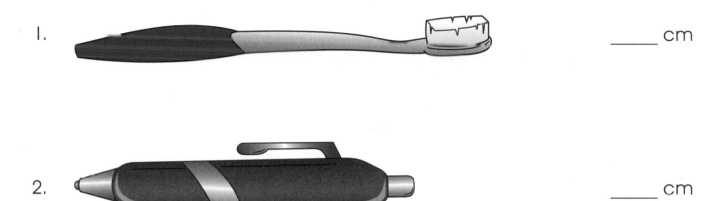

1. _____ cm

2. _____ cm

Jump for Joy and Fitness!

Build your endurance and have a hopping good time doing it! Grab a jump rope and find some happy music. Turn on the music and start jumping rope. See how long you can jump as you listen to your favorite songs. Rest in between songs based on your stamina. (Stamina just means your "staying power" or how long you can do something until you need a break.) If jumping rope is too difficult, you can still improve your endurance by jumping in place. In a few days, try again and see how many songs you can jump through. By the end of the summer, you may be able to jump through even more music, and your endurance will be better!

* See page ii.

DAY 8

Use the chart to answer each question.

Allowance for Each Chore Completed

Bundle newspapers for recycling	$0.25
Empty wastepaper baskets	$0.75
Put away groceries	$0.50
Wash the car	$2.00
Set the table	$1.00

3. Which chore pays the most money? _____

4. If Hugo sets the table for dinner every night this week, how much will

   he earn?_____

5. Davis bundled newspapers for recycling 2 times this week. How

   much money did he earn? _____

Read each statement. Write _Y_ for _yes_ or _N_ for _no_ beside each statement.

How a Snake Is Like a Turtle

6. _____ Both have shells.

7. _____ Both can be on land.

8. _____ Both are reptiles.

9. _____ Both have scales.

How a Bike Is Like a Truck

10. _____ Both have tires.

11. _____ Both need gas.

12. _____ Both can be new.

13. _____ Both have four wheels.

FACTOID: Yo-yos have ridden on at least two NASA spacecraft.

PLACE STICKER HERE

Color each shape to show the fraction.

1.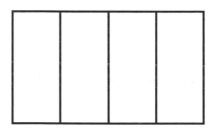
$$\frac{3}{4}$$

2.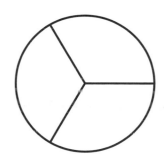
$$\frac{1}{3}$$

3.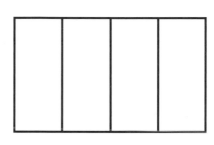
$$\frac{1}{4}$$

4.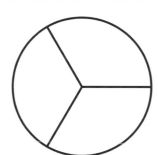
$$\frac{2}{3}$$

Write each word from the word bank under the word that has the same beginning sound.

| cake | camp | candy | center | cereal |
| circle | city | coat | corn | cent |

celery   **cat**

_____   _____

_____   _____

_____   _____

_____   _____

DAY 9

Solve each problem.

5. There are 26 students on one bus. There are 29 students on the other bus. How many students are on the buses altogether?

6. Cynthia found 47 shells on the beach. Byron found 44 shells on the beach. How many shells did they find in all?

7. Tony ran 15 laps on Monday. He ran 17 laps on Tuesday. How many laps did Tony run altogether?

8. Thomas saw 48 fish in one fish tank. Brooke saw 36 fish in another fish tank. How many fish did they see in all?

9. Write a sentence that ends with a period (.).

_____

10. Write a sentence that ends with a question mark (?).

_____

11. Write a sentence that ends with an exclamation point (!).

_____

FITNESS FLASH: Jog in place for 30 seconds.

* See page ii.

PLACE STICKER HERE

Use each fact family to write two addition and two subtraction number sentences.

1. 6, 7, 13	2. 7, 8, 15	3. 10, 7, 17
_____ + _____ = _____	_____ + _____ = _____	_____ + _____ = _____
_____ + _____ = _____	_____ + _____ = _____	_____ + _____ = _____
_____ − _____ = _____	_____ − _____ = _____	_____ − _____ = _____
_____ − _____ = _____	_____ − _____ = _____	_____ − _____ = _____
4. 6, 8, 14	5. 7, 5, 12	6. 5, 6, 11
_____ + _____ = _____	_____ + _____ = _____	_____ + _____ = _____
_____ + _____ = _____	_____ + _____ = _____	_____ + _____ = _____
_____ − _____ = _____	_____ − _____ = _____	_____ − _____ = _____
_____ − _____ = _____	_____ − _____ = _____	_____ − _____ = _____

How many sentences can you write using only the words in the word bank? Write the sentences on a separate sheet of paper.

and	at	barks	bed	big	blue	boy
car	Dad	dog	girl	I	it	little
Mom	over	parks	ran	red	small	squirrel
the	to	tree	under	up	walks	yellow

DAY 10

Use the calendars to answer each question.

			May			
S	**M**	**T**	**W**	**Th**	**F**	**S**
			1	2	3	4
5	6	7	8	9	10	11
12	13	14	15	16	17	18
19	20	21	22	23	24	25
26	27	28	29	30	31	

			June			
S	**M**	**T**	**W**	**Th**	**F**	**S**
						1
2	3	4	5	6	7	8
9	10	11	12	13	14	15
16	17	18	19	20	21	22
23	24	25	26	27	28	29
30						

7. Julia went to the dentist on the third Tuesday in May. What was the date?

Tuesday, May _____

8. Heath started his dance class on the first Monday in June. What was the date?

Monday, June _____

9. Today is May 10. Adam's family will see a play next Thursday. On what date will they see a play?

Thursday, May _____

10. How many days are between May 29 and June 5?

_____

What do you think is the most difficult part about being a parent?

_____

_____

_____

CHARACTER CHECK: Discuss with an adult how long you think it takes to regain someone's trust after telling a lie.

118

PLACE STICKER HERE

Read the poem.

Pitter-Patter

Pitter-patter, pitter-patter.
How I love the rain!

Storm clouds moving in,
The rain is about to begin.
How I love to see the rain!

Tiny sprinkles on my face,
Little droplets playing chase.
How I love to feel the rain!

I open up my mouth so wide,
Letting little drops inside.
How I love to taste the rain!

Tapping on my window,
It's a rhythm that I know.
How I love to hear the rain!

Everything looks so green,
And the fresh air smells so clean.
How I love to smell the rain!

Pitter-patter, pitter-patter.
How I love the rain!

Draw a line to match each sense with a detail in the poem.

	Sense	Detail
1.	sight	tapping a rhythm on the window
2.	touch	storm clouds moving in
3.	taste	little drops inside my mouth
4.	hearing	tiny sprinkles on my face
5.	smell	clean, fresh air

DAY 11

Write how many tens and ones.

6. 12 is the same as _____ ten and _____ ones

7. 93 is the same as _____ tens and _____ ones

8. 44 is the same as _____ tens and _____ ones

9. 76 is the same as _____ tens and _____ ones

10. 81 is the same as _____ tens and _____ one

Use the words from the word bank to complete each analogy. An analogy is a way to show how things are alike. To complete an analogy, look at the first set of words. Decide how they are related. Apply that relationship to the second set of words.

EXAMPLE: *Finger : hand :: toe : _____.* (A *finger* is part of a *hand*. What is a *toe* a part of? The answer is *foot*.)

light	sky	square	table

11. sleep : bed :: eat : _____

12. three : triangle :: four : _____

13. green : grass :: blue : _____

14. win : lose :: dark : _____

FACTOID: Dragonflies can fly at speeds of up to 40 mph (64 km/h).

PLACE STICKER HERE

Solve each problem.

EXAMPLE:

Nick left for school on the bus at 8:00.   Think: 8:00 + 0:20 = 8:20
The bus ride took 20 minutes.
What time did Nick get to school?

1. Claire ate a snack at 10:00. She ate lunch 2 hours later. What time did she eat lunch?

_____

2. This morning, Hau read for 15 minutes. He started at 9:00. What time did he finish reading?

_____

3. Recess lasted 30 minutes. It started at 2:00. What time did it end?

_____

4. Ellis left school at 3:30. He rode the bus for 30 minutes. What time did he get off of the bus?

_____

Say each word aloud. Write the syllables in the boxes.

5. apartment

6. enormous

7. subtraction

8. wonderful

DAY 12

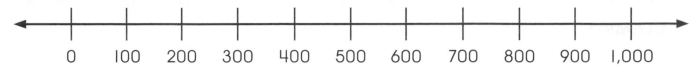

Solve each problem. Use the number line to help you add hundreds.

```
←——|——|——|——|——|——|——|——|——|——|——|——→
    0  100 200 300 400 500 600 700 800 900 1,000
```

9.   300 + 200 = _____

10.   700 + 200 = _____

11.   100 + 200 = _____

12.   600 + 400 = _____

13.   400 + 400 = _____

14.   500 + 200 = _____

Read the table of contents. Write the chapter and page number where you should begin looking for the answer to each question.

Table of Contents

15.   How long do lions live? Chapter _____ Page _____

16.   How fast do sailfish swim? Chapter _____ Page _____

17.   What color is a robin's egg? Chapter _____ Page _____

18.   Do spiders bite? Chapter _____ Page _____

FITNESS FLASH: Do 10 jumping jacks.

* See page ii.

PLACE STICKER HERE

Read the story. Fill in the table.

Today is Rachel's birthday. She invited four friends to her party. Each friend brought a gift. Rachel's brother mixed up the tags on the gifts. Can you use the clues to put the tags on the correct gifts?

Grace's gift has flowered wrapping paper and a bow.

Kate's gift is small and has a bow.

Meghan forgot to put a bow on her gift.

Jade's gift has striped wrapping paper.

Write O in the box when you know a gift was brought by the girl.
Write X in the box when you know a gift was not brought by the girl.

Kate				
Grace				
Jade				
Meghan				

If you could give any gift in the world, what would you give? Whom would you give the gift to? Write your answers on a separate sheet of paper.

DAY 13

Read the story.

Aunt Antonym

We have a nickname for my mother's sister. We call her Aunt Antonym. She always says or does the opposite of what we say or do. One day, we all went to the zoo. At the monkey exhibit, we thought the monkeys were cute. My aunt thought that they were strange. Soon, we were hungry. My aunt was still full from breakfast. After lunch, we rode the train around the zoo. My aunt wanted to walk. Finally, my aunt said that she was tired and ready to go. We were still full of energy. We wished we could have stayed.

Write _T_ next to each statement that is true. Write _F_ next to each statement that is false.

1. _____ The author is writing about his sister.

2. _____ Aunt Antonym is the real name of the author's aunt.

3. _____ Aunt Antonym was full from breakfast.

4. _____ Aunt Antonym did not want to ride the train.

Write a word from the story that is an antonym for each word.

5. ride_____ 6. stay _____

7. energetic _____ 8. hungry_____

FACTOID: A yawn lasts about six seconds.

PLACE STICKER HERE

Follow the directions to solve each problem.

1. Start with 800. Write the number that is 200 less. _____

2. Start with 600. Write the number that is 300 less. _____

3. Start with 200. Write the number that is 100 less. _____

4. Start with 700. Write the number that is 500 less. _____

5. Start with 900. Write the number that is 400 less. _____

6. Start with 600. Write the number that is 100 less. _____

Loyalty List

How can you show your loyalty this summer? Being loyal means supporting and standing up for those you love. What can you do to practice this important trait? Try making a Loyalty List. Ask an adult for a large sheet of poster board and markers. Write the things that you will do to show loyalty to those you love, such as your family and friends. Then, decorate the poster board with pictures of your friends and family. With the adult's permission, place the poster on the wall or door in your bedroom. It will help you remember how you can be loyal every day. After a week, look at your Loyalty List and write examples of how you have shown your loyalty.

DAY 14

Complete each number pattern. Write the rule.

7. 2, 4, 6, 8,_____ ,_____ ,_____ ,_____ ,_____ ,_____

    Rule: _____

8. 10, 20, 30,_____ ,_____ ,_____ ,_____ ,_____ ,_____

    Rule: _____

9. 5, 10, 15,_____ ,_____ ,_____ ,_____ ,_____ ,_____

    Rule: _____

10. 3, 6, 9, 12,_____ ,_____ ,_____ ,_____ ,_____ ,_____

    Rule: _____

Pretend that you are planning a Silly Saturday party. Write a letter to invite someone to your party.

Dear _____,

_____

_____

_____

                                    Your friend,

FITNESS FLASH: Hop on your left foot 10 times.

* See page ii.

Repeated addition problems help you get ready for multiplication. Add to find each sum.

1.	3	2.	2	3.	4	4.	5
	3		2		4		5
	+ 3		+ 2		+ 4		+ 5

5.	3	6.	2	7.	5	8.	4
	3		2		5		4
	3		2		5		4
	+ 3		+ 2		+ 5		+ 4

Write each noun in the correct column.

aunt	basement	bedroom	chair
cousin	dad	dresser	girl
lamp	restaurant	France	sink

Nouns for People	**Nouns for Places**	**Nouns for Things**
_____	_____	_____
_____	_____	_____
_____	_____	_____
_____	_____	_____

DAY 15

Write the expanded form for each number.
EXAMPLE:

251 = __2__ hundreds + __5__ tens + __1__ one = **200** + **50** + __1__

9. 341 = ____ hundreds + ____ tens + ____ one = ____ + ____ + ____

10. 563 = ____ hundreds + ____ tens + ____ ones = ____ + ____ + ____

11. 752 = ____ hundreds + ____ tens + ____ ones = ____ + ____ + ____

12. 845 = ____ hundreds + ____ tens + ____ ones = ____ + ____ + ____

Write _a_ or _an_ in front of each noun.

13. ____ lawyer   14. ____ mayor

15. ____ drummer   16. ____ officer

17. ____ author   18. ____ doctor

19. ____ diver   20. ____ scientist

21. ____ owner   22. ____ athlete

23. ____ clown   24. ____ explorer

25. ____ teacher   26. ____ artist

CHARACTER CHECK: Discuss with an adult why it is sometimes difficult to break bad habits.

PLACE STICKER HERE

Read the passage. Answer the questions.

How Plants Grow

A plant needs **energy** to grow. Energy comes from food. A plant makes its food in its leaves. Sunlight and water help the plant make food. After you plant a seed, a tiny seedling pushes its way out from the soil. The plant grows toward the sun. The plant must get water, or it will dry out and die. The roots of the plant pull water and nutrients from the soil. If there is little rain where you live, you may need to water your plant. If the soil in your area has few nutrients, you may need to add plant food to the soil. That way your plant gets what it needs.

1. What is the main idea of this passage?

 A. A plant can die without water.

 B. Plants need food, water, and sunlight to grow.

 C. Plants start as seeds.

2. What happens after you plant a seed?_____

    _____

3. Where does **energy** come from?_____

    _____

4. When might you need to water your plant? _____

    _____

DAY 16

Write a word problem for each number sentence.
EXAMPLE:

$3 + 2 = 5$ _I had 3 purple markers. My friend gave me 2 more._

Now, I have 5 purple markers.

5. $4 + 2 = 6$ _____

_____

6. $5 - 4 = 1$ _____

_____

Circle the adjective that describes each underlined noun.

7. Insects have six <u>legs</u>.

8. Bumblebees have hairy <u>bodies</u>.

9. A beetle has a hard <u>body</u>.

10. Ladybugs have black <u>spots</u>.

11. Butterflies can be beautiful <u>colors</u>.

12. Termites have powerful <u>jaws</u>.

13. Dragonflies have four <u>wings</u>.

14. A green <u>grasshopper</u> jumps away.

FACTOID: Butterflies and moths are found on every continent except Antarctica.

PLACE STICKER HERE

Circle each sentence that is in the correct order and makes sense.

1. The most common pets are cats and dogs.

   Common dogs and cats are the most pets.

2. A pet needs food, exercise, and a good place to live.

   A good place to live needs food, exercise, and pets.

3. Love pet your is the best thing you give can.

   The best thing you can give your pet is love.

Wacky Walkathon

One of the best ways to build endurance is to walk. Grab some friends or family members and get going! Find a safe place, such as a park path, school track, or nature trail. Choose a date and invite your loved ones to join you for a wacky walkathon. To make it fun, have everyone arrive wearing a costume or funny face paint. Then, get your silly group walking. Remind them that they can have fun but that they must walk fast because they are exercising! Some people may not be able to walk for as long or as fast as everyone else. That is OK as long as each walker is doing his best. Try to get the group to meet for several walkathons to get fitter and even sillier as summer goes on!

* See page ii.

DAY 17

Write each missing addend.

4.
$$\begin{array}{r} 9 \\ + \boxed{} \\ \hline 13 \end{array}$$

5.
$$\begin{array}{r} 6 \\ + \boxed{} \\ \hline 15 \end{array}$$

6.
$$\begin{array}{r} 9 \\ + \boxed{} \\ \hline 18 \end{array}$$

7.
$$\begin{array}{r} 4 \\ + \boxed{} \\ \hline 13 \end{array}$$

8.
$$\begin{array}{r} 4 \\ + \boxed{} \\ \hline 10 \end{array}$$

9.
$$\begin{array}{r} 7 \\ + \boxed{} \\ \hline 16 \end{array}$$

10.
$$\begin{array}{r} 7 \\ + \boxed{} \\ \hline 11 \end{array}$$

11.
$$\begin{array}{r} 6 \\ + \boxed{} \\ \hline 14 \end{array}$$

12.
$$\begin{array}{r} 8 \\ + \boxed{} \\ \hline 17 \end{array}$$

13.
$$\begin{array}{r} 8 \\ + \boxed{} \\ \hline 12 \end{array}$$

14.
$$\begin{array}{r} 5 \\ + \boxed{} \\ \hline 11 \end{array}$$

15.
$$\begin{array}{r} 9 \\ + \boxed{} \\ \hline 18 \end{array}$$

Read the story.

Winter Fun

Some people like spring, but I do not. I think that winter is the best season. My family goes to the mountains every year. My stepmom is a good skier. She skis while we watch. My dad wears snowshoes and goes on long walks. My brothers and I like to play in the snow. The nights are too cold to be outside. So, we stay warm in our cabin. My stepmom makes us hot chocolate at bedtime, and we tell stories.

Decide whether each sentence is a fact or an opinion. Write _F_ for fact or _O_ for opinion.

16. _____ Winter is the best season.

17. _____ My family goes to the mountains.

18. _____ My stepmom makes us hot chocolate.

19. _____ I think my stepmom is a good skier.

20. _____ The nights are too cold.

21. _____ Dad goes on long walks.

FITNESS FLASH: Hop on your right foot for 30 seconds.

* See page ii.

PLACE STICKER HERE

Read the passage. Answer the questions.

The Moon

The moon lights up the night sky. Sometimes, the moon looks narrow. Sometimes, it looks round. The appearance of the moon has to do with the position of the moon as viewed from Earth. When the moon is between the sun and Earth, the moon looks black. This is called a new moon. When Earth is between the sun and the moon, the moon looks bright and round. This is called a full moon. In the middle of these periods, half of the moon is lit, and half of the moon is dark. It takes about one month for the moon to finish the entire cycle.

1. What is the main idea of this passage?

    A. The moon can look thin or fat.

    B. The moon travels around Earth.

    C. The moon looks different throughout the month.

2. What makes the moon's appearance change? _____

_____

3. When does a new moon happen? _____

_____

4. When does a full moon happen? _____

_____

DAY 18

Circle the two bugs in each box with equal differences.

5.   7 – 2   7 – 5

   5 – 3

6.   9 – 8   5 – 2

   4 – 3

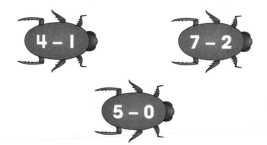

7.   4 – 1   7 – 2

   5 – 0

8.   6 – 6   9 – 9

   4 – 2

Read the story.

Learning to Cook

My brother is helping me learn to cook. I think he is an excellent cook. Last night, we made noodles with tomato sauce. We also made spinach bread. We planned to bake a pie, but we ran out of flour. Mom loved the meal. She said, "You're hired!"

Decide whether each sentence is a fact or an opinion. Write _F_ for fact or _O_ for opinion.

9. _____ I think my brother is an excellent cook.

10. _____ We ran out of flour.

11. _____ We made spinach bread.

12. _____ Pie is good.

FACTOID: Benjamin Franklin started the first lending library.

134

PLACE STICKER HERE

Read the passage. Answer the questions.

Teeth

Teeth are important for chewing food, so you need to take care of your teeth. When you are a child, you have baby teeth. These fall out and are replaced by adult teeth. You can expect to have 32 teeth one day. You should brush your teeth at least twice a day—once in the morning and once at bedtime. Also, you should floss to remove food that gets stuck between your teeth. That way, you will have a healthy smile!

1. What is the main idea of this passage?

    A. You can have a healthy smile.

    B. It is important to take care of your teeth.

    C. Adults have more teeth than children.

2. Why should you take care of your teeth? _____

    _____

3. What happens to baby teeth? _____

    _____

4. How many teeth do adults have? _____

5. How often should you brush your teeth?

    A. only at lunchtime

    B. at least once a week

    C. at least twice a day

DAY 19

Subtract to find each difference.

6.	63 − 40	7.	80 − 60	8.	75 − 50	9.	79 − 20	10.	38 − 10	11.	93 − 30

12.	67 − 40	13.	83 − 20	14.	77 − 10	15.	76 − 50	16.	59 − 30	17.	77 − 60

Write *to*, *too*, or *two* to finish each sentence.

18. Are you checking out _____ books?

19. Is your birthday today _____?

20. Amber is going _____ the ballet tonight.

21. The muffins are _____ hot to eat right now.

22. Please hand those _____ Becca.

23. I am riding my bike _____ the park.

24. That shirt was small, so I gave it _____ Paul.

25. My brother will be _____ years old on Friday.

FITNESS FLASH: Jog in place for 30 seconds.

* See page ii.

PLACE
STICKER
HERE

Tara and her dad planted a tiny pine tree in their yard on her sixth birthday. They measured it every year on her birthday to see how many inches it had grown. Look at the graph and answer the questions.

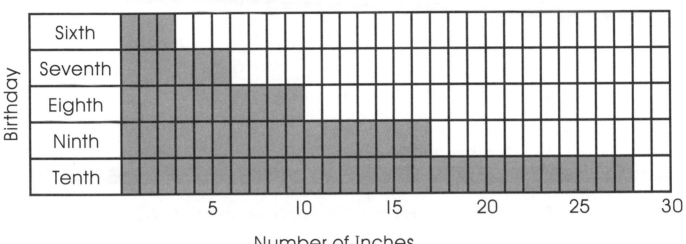

Growth of Tara's Pine Tree

1. How tall was the tree when Tara planted it? _____

2. How tall was the tree on Tara's eighth birthday? _____

3. On which birthday was the tree 17 inches tall? _____

4. How many inches did the tree grow from Tara's seventh birthday to

    her eighth birthday? _____

5. How many inches did the tree grow from Tara's ninth birthday to her

    tenth birthday? _____

6. How many inches did the tree grow from Tara's seventh birthday to

    her ninth birthday? _____

DAY 20

Circle the number sentences that are true.

7. $7 = 7$

8. $8 > 5$

9. $7 = 8$

10. $9 < 7$

11. $4 + 3 = 7$

12. $6 = 4 + 3$

13. $2 + 3 = 5$

14. $2 = 1 + 1$

15. $7 + 4 = 3$

16. $9 = 3 + 6$

17. $5 + 2 = 5 + 2$

18. $4 + 3 = 3 + 4$

19. $4 + 6 = 5 + 3$

20. $5 + 6 = 10$

Which part of speech is underlined in each sentence? Write *noun*, *verb*, or *adjective*.

21. I <u>comb</u> the tangles out of my hair. _____

22. Riley has a red <u>comb</u>. _____

23. Cassidy likes <u>cherry</u> pie. _____

24. I want to eat that <u>cherry</u>. _____

25. The fruit <u>bat</u> hangs upside down to sleep. _____

26. Felipe and Joe <u>bat</u> the ball over the fence. _____

27. Turn on the <u>light</u>. _____

28. Gerry carried the <u>light</u> bag. _____

> **CHARACTER CHECK:** Discuss with an adult what you can do when you are being bullied.

138

PLACE STICKER HERE

Catching Ice Cubes

Can you use salt and a piece of string to "catch" an ice cube?

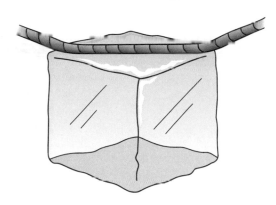

Materials:
- ice cube
- salt
- string

Procedure:
1. Try to catch the ice cube with the piece of string. (You cannot tie the string around the ice cube.) Can you do it?

2. Next, place the string on the ice cube and sprinkle a little salt on the string. Count to 30 and slowly lift the string. The ice cube will be attached!

What's This All About?

When you sprinkle salt on the ice, it lowers the freezing temperature of the ice. This causes some water to melt around the string. When the water forms, it dilutes the salt on the ice and allows the water to freeze around the string. This is why you can pick it up.

Pinching Water

Can you hold two streams of water together? Or, can you separate two streams of water that had been flowing together? You would probably have to be pretty powerful! Or, would you?

Materials:
- nail (8- or 16-penny)
- hammer
- soup can (empty)
- water
- masking tape

Procedure:

1. Ask an adult to use a hammer and nail to make two small holes in the lower section of the soup can. The holes should be close to the bottom and 0.5 inches (1.27 cm) apart. Tape over the holes.

2. Fill the can with water and hold it over a sink. Then, remove the tape.

3. Using your fingers, try to pinch the two streams of water together.

4. Using your fingers, try to split the two streams of water.

What's This All About?

When you pinch the streams of water together, the water molecules act like magnets. They attract each other and form larger water drops.

By splitting the water streams, you push the streams far enough away that they cannot attract each other. So, they stay separate. As long as you have water in the can, you will be able to pinch or split the streams of water.

Animals Around the World

Studying animals is a great way to learn about different places in the world. Go to the library and check out books about animals that live in other parts of the world. Or, search the Internet with an adult to find out about animals. Choose an animal that lives on each continent (Africa, Antarctica, Asia, Australia, Europe, North America, and South America). As you read about each animal, you may find that the climate (weather patterns) or the food that grows in a place affects which animals live there. On the chart, write the name of each animal, the continent on which it lives, and why it lives there.

ANIMAL	CONTINENT	WHY IT LIVES THERE

Dessert Map

A relief map shows the physical features of a place, such as rivers and mountains. Sometimes it is called a topographical map. You will call this a delicious map when you are finished with this activity!

Make this map in the kitchen with an adult's help. You will need two packages of prepared sugar cookie dough. You will also need some toppings, such as chocolate syrup, sliced fruit, and sprinkles.

Press the cookie dough from one package onto a cookie sheet. Use the other package of cookie dough to mold and shape land features. You could make mountains, hills, islands, volcanoes, deserts, forests, and valleys.

Bake the "map," following the directions on the package. Let the map cool. Use chocolate syrup to make water features, such as lakes and rivers. Highlight other features with different toppings.

Share the dessert with your family. Tell them what you learned about relief maps.

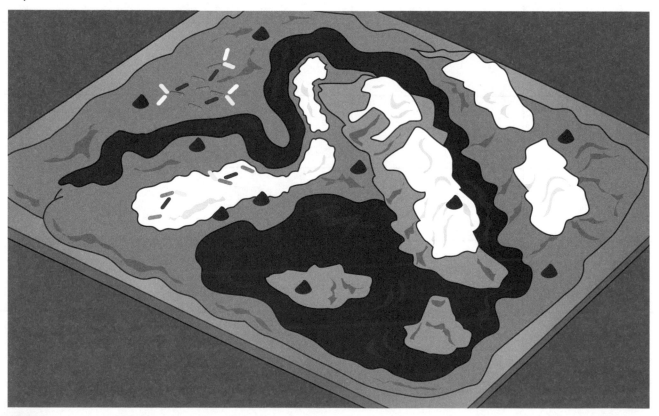

* See page ii.

Earth Effects

The earth is a big place. Did you know that what you do every day can affect the earth? Almost every human action does something to the earth. Think about this: If a family goes to the beach for the day and leaves behind a few soft drink cans, a newspaper, and an empty sunscreen bottle, they have had a negative effect on the earth. But, if they had simply taken the items with them and dropped them off in recycling bins, they would have had a positive effect on the earth. The metal cans, plastic holder, and sunscreen bottle could be recycled and made into something new. Trash would not have littered the beach. The ocean animals would not have been hurt by the trash left behind.

Do you want to have a positive effect on the earth? Have your family members help you make a list of things you can do to be good to the earth.

_____

_____

_____

_____

_____

_____

_____

BONUS

Take It Outside!

Collect several different small outdoor objects: a pinecone, a leaf, a flower, a nut, a rock, and other safe, interesting outdoor things. Put each item on the ground. Look at each item. Decide whether each item is symmetrical. *Symmetrical* means that if you cut something in half, the two sides will look the same and have the same parts. If they do, then the object is symmetrical. If they do not, then the object is asymmetrical.

Pick up a notebook and pencil. Now, take a walk. As you go, write 10 things you see. Then, write two words to describe each thing. This is good practice for writing adjectives and a great way to take a look at nature.

When you are outside, list the things you see, such as the names on your neighbors' mailboxes. Practice putting the names in ABC order. As you improve, make the list longer to include many outside objects. Challenge yourself to find something that starts with each letter of the alphabet. Good luck with *Q* and *X*!

* See page ii.

Section I

Day 1: 1. The parrots should be matched to their places in line; 2. b; 3. n; 4. b; 5. r; 6. t; 7. r; The capital letters should be written from A to Z; 8. o; 9. a; 10. e; 11. u; 12. i; 13. o

Day 2: 1. 4; 2. 2; 3. 1; 4. 8; 5. 6; 6. 10; 7. 6; 8. 6; 9. 4; 10. 8; 11. 3; 12. 7; 13. v; 14. b; 15. f; 16. t; 17. g; 18. k; The lowercase letters should be written from a to z; 19. Drawings will vary.

Day 3:

1. ;

2. ; 3. 6:00;

4. ; 5. 12:00;

6. ; 7. e; 8. i; 9. o;

10. a; 11. a; 12. i; 13. C, B, D, A; 14. tape; 15. mop; 16. slide

Day 4: 1. 3, 4, 7, 8, 11, 12, 15, 16, 19, 20, 23, 24; 2. 32, 33, 35, 36, 38, 39, 41, 42, 44, 45, 47, 48, 50; 3. 75, 76, 79, 80, 81, 83, 84, 86, 87, 88, 90, 91, 93, 94, 96, 97, 99, 100, 101; 4. can; 5. pan; 6. pin; 7. cube; 8. kite; 9. cap; Students should write their first and last names;

10. ?; 11. ?; 12. .; 13. .; 14. ?; 15. ?; 16. !; 17. !; 18. .; 19. ?

Day 5: 1. 4¢; 2. 22¢; 3. 26¢; 4. 25¢; 5. 61¢; 6. o; 7. u; 8. a; 9. e; 10. a; 11. i; 12. hat, bat, sat; 13. rag, tag, sag; 14. she, me, we, see; 15. rake, lake, make, bake; 16. ring, thing, wing; 17. fun, sun, spun; 18. Check the drawing. Titles will vary.

Day 6: 1. 24; 2. 40; 3. 33; 4. 57; 5. 26; 6. 45; 7. e; 8. a; 9. i; 10. e; 11. u; 12. o; 13. in—out; 14. up—down; 15. big—little; 16. tall—short; 17. soft—hard; 18. hot—cold; 19. off—on; 20. happy—sad

Day 7: 1. 9 train cars; 2. 4 deer; 3. 7 words; 4. 10 markers; 5. it's; 6. they've; 7. we'll; 8. I'm; 9. you'll; 10. she'll; 11. apple, book, cat; 12. dog, eagle, fish; 13. girl, hat, ice; 14. king, lamp, map; 15. bow; 16. eye; 17. sun

Day 8: 1. 18¢; 2. 13¢; 3. 12¢; 4. 17¢; 5. 24¢; 6. 37¢; 7.–9. Answers will vary; 10. dark; 11. girls; 12. hop; 13. wet; Answers will vary.

Day 9:

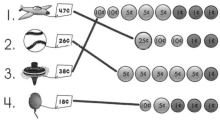

5. 2 in.; 6. 6 in.; 7. D; 8. B; 9. ?; 10. .; 11. ?; 12. ?

Day 10: 1. 11; 2. 4; 3. 10; 4. 5; 5. 11; 6. 6; 7. 11; 8. 6; 9. 11; 10. 6; 11. 11; 12. 11; 13. 12; 14. 10; 15. 2; 16. doctor; 17. farmer; 18. pilot; 19. teacher; 20. baker; The following words should be colored blue: try, tie, light, my, sigh, try, bike, sign, pie, guy, by, high, dry, bite, time, night, cry, dime, fine, lie, sight, why, right, shy, ride, buy, side, hike, kite, nine; The following words should be colored green: bib, wig, six, if, fib, gift, pit, miss, fish, lit, chin, sit, hill, hid, bill, quit, bin, mitt, tin, win, fit, will, pin, fin, zip, did; 21. backed, baked; 22. whent, went; 23. trane, train; 24. rom, room

Day 11: 1. 5, 2, 3, 5; 2. 9, 2, 7, 2; 3. 8, 3, 5, 5, 3, 8, 5; 4. white; 5. brown; 6. purple; 7. blue; 8. green; 9. orange; 10. yellow; 11. black; 12. red; 13. pink; 14. C; 15. 2, 1, 3

Day 12: 1. 4; 2. 12; 3. 2; 4. 16; 5. 4; 6. 9; 7. 14; 8. 6; 9. 9; 10. 5; 11. 2; 12. 6; 13. 11; 14. 5; 15. 7; 16. dr; 17. tr; 18. gr; 19. cl; 20. gl; 21. st; 22. it's—it is; 23. we're—we are; 24. you've—you have; 25. don't — do not; 26. we'll—we will; 27. isn't—is not; 28. Ducks like to swim.; 29. Can we play in the sandbox?; 30. Some birds make nests in trees.; 31. Are you having fun today?

Day 13: I. 7 cm; 2. 14 cm; Students should circle the cake, whale, gate, and grapes; 3. cookbook; 4. baseball; 5. butterfly; 6. firefighter; 7. red; 8. blue; 9. red; 10. blue

Day 14: I. 9, 9, 4, 5; 2. 2, 6, 8, 6, 2, 6; 3. Answers will vary but may include: 7, 3, 10, 3, 7, 10, 10, 7, 3, 10, 3, 7; 4. t, n; 5. s, n; 6. c, t; 7. n, t; 8. l, p; 9. c, n; 10. C; 11. B; 12. when; 13. who; 14. where; 15. what; 16. where

Day 15: I. 6 baseballs; 2. 4 apples; Answers will vary; 3. C; 4. 3, 1, 2

Day 16: I. circle; 2. triangle; 3. oval; 4. pentagon; 5. cat or rat; 6. toys; 7. The bee is on the flower; 8. The bird is on the bowl; 9. 2; 10. 1; 11. 1; 12. 2

Day 17: I. 30, 50, 60, 80, 90; 2. 20, 25, 30, 45, 50, 60, 65, 75, 80, 85, 95, 100; 3. 6, 10, 14, 16, 20, 24, 28, 30, 34, 36, 38, 40, 44; 4. a; 5. o; 6. u; 7. a; 8. i; 9. i; 10. on top of; 11. next to; 12. under; long a: great, break, steak; long e: peach, leaf, beat

Day 18: I. 4, 1; 2. 4, 5; 3. 8, 4; 4. 6, 5; 5. 7, 2; 6. 1, 7; 7. 3, 9; 8. 5, 0; 9. 5, 1; 10. 9, 7; 11. 10, 0; 12. last—fast; 13. bee—tree; 14. sand—band; 15. blue—glue; 16. chair—hair; 17. mean—bean; 18. main—rain; 19. 4; 20. 2; 21. 5; 22. 3; 23. 1; Answers and drawings will vary.

Day 19: I. <; 2. >; 3. <; 4. >; 5. >; 6. >; 7. >; 8. <; 9. <; 10. <; 11. >; 12. >; 13. <; 14. <; 15. >; end–finish, small–little, hear–listen, happy–glad, below–under; 16. ant; 17. baby; 18. key; 19. dog

Day 20:

I.  ; 2. 4:00;

3.  ; 4. 11:00;

5.  ; 6. 8:30;

7. ch; 8. wh; 9. sh; 10. 2 in.; 11. 4 in.; 12. C; 13. A; 14. B

Section II

Day I: I. I cookie; 2. 3 bananas; 3. 3 rabbits; 4. 3 flowers; 5.–6. Answers will vary; 7. The sun will shine today.; 8. I walked a mile today.; 9. We painted our fence.; 10. She will knit something for me.; 11. big; 12. fast; 13. go; 14. little; 15. out; 16. slow; 17. stop; 18. up

Day 2: I. 71; 2. 91; 3. 72; 4. 34; 5. 41; 6. 40; 7. 99; 8. 80; 9. 54; 10. glue; 11. frog; 12. clock; 13. bowl; 14. C; 15. B; 16. hands; 17. kittens; 18. glasses; 19. inches; 20. cars; 21. clocks; 22. wishes; 23. brushes

Day 3: I. 48¢; 2. 62¢; 3. 39¢; 4. 25¢; 5. 12; 6. 12; 7. 10; 8. 14; 9. 17; 10. 16; 11. 4; 12. 5; 13. 4; 14. 0; 15. 8; 16. 4; 17. rake; 18. tag; 19. call; 20. gate

Day 4: I. 4, 6; 2. 1, 9; 3. 8, 4; 4. 6, 4; 5. 40; 6. 11; 7. 93; 8. 28; The other half of the flower should be drawn; 9.–14. Students should draw an X on each correct shape; 15. you; 16. give; 17. sit; 18. mix

Day 5: Answers will vary; Answers will vary; I. Olivia lives on a farm.; 2. Olivia wakes up early to do chores.; 3. Answers will vary but may include: Olivia feeds the horses and the chickens, collects the eggs, and helps milk the cows; 4. Olivia's favorite thing to do in the morning is eat breakfast; 5. oi; 6. oi; 7. oi

Day 6: I. 6; 2. 3; 3. 12; 4. 15; 5. 7; 6. 7; 7. 14; 8. 9; 9. 15; 10. 12; 11. 14; 12. 30;

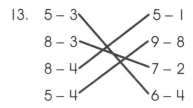

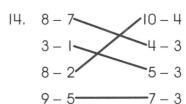

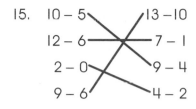

15.
10 – 5   13 –10
12 – 6   7 – 1
2 – 0   9 – 4
9 – 6   4 – 2

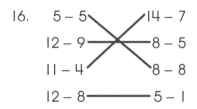

16.
5 – 5   14 – 7
12 – 9   8 – 5
11 – 4   8 – 8
12 – 8   5 – 1

17. gift, his; 18. car, flat; 19. sat, the; 20. dad, store

Day 7: 1. Sidney's umbrella is old; 2. Tabby is a farm cat; 3. It is going to snow; 4. dirty; 5. day; 6. cold; 7. dark; 8. cry;

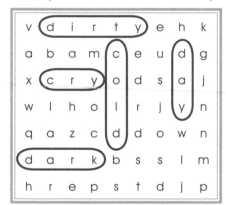

9. yes; 10. no; 11. yes; 12. e, i, e, e, i; 13. i, e, i, e, e; 14. i, i, e, e, i

Day 8: 1. book; 2. leg; 3. cat; 4. chair; 5. apple; 6. Tom; 7. park; 8. basket; 9. oy, boy; 10. oy, toy; 11. oi, soil; 12. oi, point; 13. oy, oyster; 14. oi, voice; 15. A; 16. B; 17. B

Day 9: 1. sang; 2. ring; 3. is; 4. ran; 5. take; 6. has; Answers will vary; 7. 28¢; 8. 25 stamps;

9. 28 fish; 10. 23 balloons; 11. frog; 12. land; 13. stone; 14. glad; 15. most; 16. crop; 17. swim; 18. sled

Day 10: 1. 53; 2. 97; 3. 30; 4. 57; 5. 78; 6. 79; 7. sh; 8. th; 9. ch; 10. 8, 10, 12; 11. 8, 16, 20, 24; 12. 10, 20, 25; 13. far; 14. no; 15. go

Day 11: 1. eight; 2. hear; 3. sea; 4. bee; 5. wood; 6. right; 7. through; 8. knot; Answers will vary; Answers will vary but may include trap, pin, car, map, can, and trim; 9. gold/fish; 10. pop/corn; 11. day/time; 12. dog/house; 13. space/ship; 14. rail/road; 15. blue/berry; 16. sail/boat; 17. grape/fruit; 18. cup/cake; 19. news/paper; 20. some/time

Day 12: 1. 8; 2. 1; 3. 3; 4. 9; 5. 2; 6. 4; 7. 7; 8. 2; 9. 4; 10. 9; 11. 3; 12. 7; 13. 8; 14. 10; 15. 3; 16. 11; 17. 4; 18. 5; 19. *Large* should be underlined and *little* should be circled; 20. *Quick* should be underlined and *slow* should be underlined and *sad* should be circled; 21. *Happy* should be underlined and *sad* should be circled; 22. *Grin* should be underlined and *frown* should be circled; 23. *Bright* should be underlined and *cloudy* should be circled; 24. 2; 25. 3; 26. 4; 27. 1

Day 13: 1. 23; 2. 46; 3. 18; 4. 54; 5. 39; 6. 67; 7. pet;

8. barn; 9. help; 10. wet; 11. boy, shoe; 12. She, letter, aunt; 13. you, sandwich; 14. We, movie, butterflies; 15. sister, teddy bear; January, February, March, April, May, June, July, August, September, October, November, December

Day 14: 1. 5, 7, 3, 9, 11; 2. 1, 7, 13, 15, 17; 3. 5, 11, 9, 13, 17, 19, 3; 4. 6, 2, 4, 8, 12; 5. 8, 10, 6, 12, 16; 6. 14, 16, 12, 18, 4, 8; 7. m; 8. v; 9. g; 10. d; 11. m; 12. l; 13. coin; 14. toy; 15. paw; 16. daughter; Answers and drawings will vary.

Day 15: 1. The ferrets lived in the American West; 2. The scientists worked to save the ferrets; 3. The number of ferrets increased after the scientists started working to save them; 4. C; 5. B; 6. 1, 0, 1; 7. 1, 4, 3; 8. 1, 9, 11; 9. 9, 3, 2; 10. can't; 11. I'm; 12. you're; 13. don't; 14. he's; 15. I'll; 16. did not; 17. is not; 18. you have; 19. she is; 20. could not; 21. we are

Day 16: 1. are; 2. is; 3. is; 4. are; 5. Is; 6. Are; Answers will vary; Answers will vary; 7. ?; 8. !; 9. !; 10. ?; 11. .; 12. 11; 13. 12; 14. 8; 15. 14; 16. 9; 17. 6; 18. 11; 19. 7; 20. 2; 21. 11; 22. start; 23. close; 24. ill; 25. angry; 26. happy; 27. tidy; 28. big; 29. quick; 30. scared; 31. funny

Day 17: 1. zebra; 2. flown; 3. bowl; 4. zipper; 5. people; 6. today; 7. shoes; 8. 10; 9. 13; 10. 13; 11. 8; 12. 11; 13. 10; 14. 12; 15. 10; 16. 10; 17. 11; 18. 7; 19. 13; 20. small; 21. automobile; 22. glad; 23. rush

Day 18: 1. One-half of the shape should be colored; 2. One-third of the shape should be colored; 3. One-fourth of the shape should be colored;

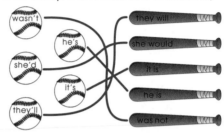

4. 78; 5. 49; 6. 39; 7. 50; 8. 15; 9. 96; 10. 28; 11. 61; 12. 88; 13. 76; 14. 41; 15. 69; 16. bird; 17. cake; 18. bone; 19. bell; 20. bring; 21. think; 22. noon; 23. happy; 24. easy; 25. body

Day 19: 1. oak; 2. six; 3. funny; 4. red; 5. hard; 6. furry; 7. A; 8. A; 9. Two nickels should be circled; 10. A penny, a nickel, and a dime should be circled; 11. Two dimes and a nickel should be circled; 12. Four dimes and a nickel should be circled; 13. ate—eight; 14. cent—sent; 15. our—hour; 16. won—one; 17. knew—new; 18. pair—pear; 19. hear—here; 20. know—no; 21. right—write; 22. blew—blue

Day 20: 1. 6; 2. 4; 3. 4; 4. 12; 5. 10; 6. 2; 7. 5; 8. 10; 9. 19; 10. 2; 11. 14; 12. 12; 13. 13; 14. strong—weak; 15. bad—good; 16. over—under; 17. old—new; 18. happy—sad; 19. add—subtract; 20. wet—dry; 21. always—never; 22. light—dark; 23. slow—fast; 24. tall—short; 25. on—off; 26. inside—outside; 27. float—sink; Check the drawing; Answers will vary.

Section III

Day 1: 1. 18, 17, 19, 13, 14; 2. 10, 14, 12, 15, 11, 13; 3. 16, 12, 14, 13, 10, 11; 4. can't; 5. easy; 6. key; 7. buy; 8. light; 9. once; 10. carry; 11. you're; 12. star; 13. funny; 14. 5 + 8 = 13, 13 − 8 = 5, 13 − 5 = 8; 15. 5 + 7 = 12, 7 + 5 = 12, 12 − 7 = 5, 12 − 5 = 7; 16. 8 + 6 = 14, 6 + 8 = 14, 14 − 8 = 6, 14 − 6 = 8; The following words should be written under *nose*: coat, drove, rope, those; The following words should be written under *pop*: rock, fox, job, top.

Day 2: 1. 0, 2, 5, 6, 3; 2. 7, 6, 4, 5, 3, 8; 3. 9, 5, 7, 3, 6, 4; 4. ir; 5. or; 6. ar; 7. ur; 8. or; 9. ar; 10. 9 miles; 11. 9 miles; 12. no; 13. no; 14. yes; 15. no; 16. yes; 17. no; 18. no

Day 3: 1. 36; 2. 39; 3. 58; 4. 69; 5. 23; 6. 99; 7. 39; 8. 105; 9. 80; 10. 98; 11. 49; 12. 79; 13. 99; 14. 59; 15. 52;

16. j; 17. j; 18. g; 19. g; 20. g; 21. j; 22. j; 23. j; 24. g; 25. 0 hundreds, 4 tens, 8 ones, 48; 26. 1 hundred, 4 tens, 4 ones, 144; 27. 1 hundred, 1 ten, 5 ones, 115; 28. 1 hundred, 3 tens, 7 ones, 137; 29. Answers will vary.

Day 4: 1. 96; 2. 21; 3. 82; 4. 37; 5. 65; 6. 61; 7. 79; 8. 58; 9. 22; 10. 80; 11. 18; 12. 100; 13. F; 14. G; 15. E; 16. B; 17. A; 18. J; 19. D; 20. I; 21. H; 22. C; 23. big—little; 24. slow—fast; 25. white—black; 26. This poem is about a missing cat; 27. The cat is big, it has black spots, and it runs fast.

Day 5: 1. 23; 2. 57; 3. 52; 4. 26; 5. 39; 6. 10; The following words should be written under *cow*: how, brown, clown, tower, crown; The following words should be written under *pillow*: blow, elbow, bowl, mow, own; 7. A; 8. E; 9. F; 10. C; 11. B; 12. D; Answers will vary.

Day 6: 1. +2; 2. −2; 3. +10; 4. −1; 5. ck; 6. gr; 7. sh; 8. sh; 9. sl; 10. ng; 11. A; 12. A philatelist is a person who collects stamps.

Day 7: 1. 1/4; 2. 2/3; 3. 1/2; 4. fireworks; 5. grandfather; 6. cartwheel; 7. sunflower; 8. snowflakes; 9. waterfall; 10. 11, 9, 15, 17 (circled); 11. 16, 9, 18 (circled), 12; 12. 9, 10, 13, 16 (circled); 13. 11, 4, 14 (circled), 13; 14. B, C

Day 8: 1. 11 cm; 2. 9 cm; 3. wash the car; 4. $7.00; 5. $0.50; 6. N; 7. Y; 8. Y; 9. N; 10. Y; 11. N; 12. Y; 13. N

Day 9: 1. Three-fourths of the shape should be colored; 2. One-third of the shape should be colored; 3. One-fourth of the shape should be colored; 4. Two-thirds of the shape should be colored; The following words should be written under *celery*: circle, city, center, cereal, cent.; The following words should be written under *cat*: cake, camp, candy, coat, corn; 5. 55 students; 6. 91 shells; 7. 32 laps; 8. 84 fish; 9.–11. Answers will vary.

Day 10: 1. 6 + 7 = 13, 7 + 6 = 13, 13 – 7 = 6, 13 – 6 = 7; 2. 7 + 8 = 15, 8 + 7 = 15, 15 – 8 = 7, 15 – 7 = 8; 3. 10 + 7 = 17, 7 + 10 = 17, 17 – 10 = 7, 17 – 7 = 10; 4. 6 + 8 = 14, 8 + 6 = 14, 14 – 8 = 6, 14 – 6 = 8; 5. 7 + 5 = 12, 5 + 7 = 12, 12 – 7 = 5, 12 – 5 = 7; 6. 5 + 6 = 11, 6 + 5 = 11, 11 – 6 = 5, 11 – 5 = 6; Answers will vary; 7. 21; 8. 3; 9. 16; 10. 6; Answers will vary.

Day 11: 1. sight—storm clouds moving in; 2. touch—tiny sprinkles on my face; 3. taste—little drops inside my mouth; 4. hearing—tapping a rhythm on the window; 5. smell—clean, fresh air; 6. 1, 2; 7. 9, 3; 8. 4, 4; 9. 7, 6; 10. 8, 1; 11. table; 12. square; 13. sky; 14. light

Day 12: 1. 12:00; 2. 9:15; 3. 2:30; 4. 4:00; 5. a/part/ment; 6. e/nor/mous; 7. sub/trac/tion; 8. won/der/ful; 9. 500; 10. 900; 11. 300; 12. 1,000; 13. 800; 14. 700; 15. 1, 3; 16. 4, 35; 17. 6, 57; 18. 5, 49

Day 13:

Kate	X	X	X	O
Grace	X	O	X	X
Jade	O	X	X	X
Meghan	X	X	O	X

Answers will vary; 1. F; 2. F; 3. T; 4. T; 5. walk; 6. go; 7. tired; 8. full

Day 14: 1. 600; 2. 300; 3. 100; 4. 200; 5. 500; 6. 500; 7. 10, 12, 14, 16, 18, 20, +2; 8. 40, 50, 60, 70, 80, 90, +10; 9. 20, 25, 30, 35, 40, 45, +5; 10. 15, 18, 21, 24, 27, 30, +3; Answers will vary.

Day 15: 1. 9; 2. 6; 3. 12; 4. 15; 5. 12; 6. 8; 7. 20; 8. 16; The following words should be written under *Nouns for People*: aunt, cousin, dad, girl; The following words should be written under *Nouns for Places*: basement, restaurant, bedroom, France; The following words should be written under *Nouns for Things*: lamp, dresser, chair, sink; 9. 3, 4, 1, 300 + 40 + 1; 10. 5, 6, 3, 500 + 60 + 3; 11. 7, 5, 2, 700 + 50 + 2; 12. 8, 4, 5, 800 + 40 + 5; 13. a; 14. a; 15. a; 16. an; 17. an; 18. a; 19. a; 20. a; 21. an; 22. an; 23. a; 24. an; 25. a; 26. an

Day 16: 1. B; 2. After you plant a seed, a tiny seedling pushes its way out; 3. Energy comes from food; 4. You might need to water your plant if there is little rain where you live; 5.–6. Answers will vary; 7. six; 8. hairy; 9. hard; 10. black; 11. beautiful; 12. powerful; 13. four; 14. green

Day 17: 1. The most common pets are cats and dogs; 2. A pet needs food, exercise, and a good place to live; 3. The best thing you can give your pet is love; 4. 4; 5. 9; 6. 9; 7. 9; 8. 6; 9. 9; 10. 4; 11. 8; 12. 9; 13. 4; 14. 6; 15. 9; 16. O; 17. F; 18. F; 19. O; 20. O; 21. F

Day 18: 1. C; 2. The position of the moon as viewed from Earth makes the moon's appearance change; 3. A new moon happens when the moon is between the sun and the earth; 4. A full moon happens when the earth is between the sun and the moon; 5. The bugs with 7 – 5 and 5 – 3 should be circled; 6. The bugs with 9 – 8 and 4 – 3 should be circled; 7. The bugs with 7 – 2 and 5 – 0 should be circled; 8. The bugs with 6 – 6 and 9 – 9 should be circled; 9. O; 10. F; 11. F; 12. O

Day 19: 1. B; 2. You should take care of your teeth because teeth are important for chewing food; 3. Baby teeth fall out and are replaced by adult teeth; 4. 32 teeth; 5. C; 6. 23; 7. 20; 8. 25; 9. 59; 10. 28; 11. 63; 12. 27; 13. 63; 14. 67; 15. 26; 16. 29; 17. 17; 18. two; 19. too; 20. to; 21. too; 22. to; 23. to; 24. to; 25. two

Day 20: 1. 3 inches; 2. 10 inches; 3. ninth; 4. 4 inches; 5. 11 inches; 6. 11 inches; The following number sentences should be circled: 7, 8, 11, 13, 14, 16, 17, 18; 21. verb; 22. noun; 23. adjective; 24. noun; 25. noun; 26. verb; 27. noun; 28. adjective

addend	adjective	amount
antonym	attempt	cause
complete	correct	difference

effect

© Carson-Dellosa

energy

© Carson-Dellosa

event

© Carson-Dellosa

fact

© Carson-Dellosa

fraction

© Carson-Dellosa

habitat

© Carson-Dellosa

homophone

© Carson-Dellosa

length

© Carson-Dellosa

map

© Carson-Dellosa

opinion	opposite	passage
© Carson-Dellosa	© Carson-Dellosa	© Carson-Dellosa
pattern	rhyme	rhythm
© Carson-Dellosa	© Carson-Dellosa	© Carson-Dellosa
sentence	solve	struggle
© Carson-Dellosa	© Carson-Dellosa	© Carson-Dellosa

subtract

sum

vanish

$$\begin{array}{r} 1 \\ +\ 1 \\ \hline \end{array}$$

$$\begin{array}{r} 2 \\ +\ 1 \\ \hline \end{array}$$

$$\begin{array}{r} 3 \\ +\ 1 \\ \hline \end{array}$$

$$\begin{array}{r} 4 \\ +\ 1 \\ \hline \end{array}$$

$$\begin{array}{r} 5 \\ +\ 1 \\ \hline \end{array}$$

$$\begin{array}{r} 6 \\ +\ 1 \\ \hline \end{array}$$

7 + 1	8 + 1	9 + 1
© Carson-Dellosa	© Carson-Dellosa	© Carson-Dellosa
2 + 2	3 + 2	4 + 2
© Carson-Dellosa	© Carson-Dellosa	© Carson-Dellosa
5 + 2	6 + 2	7 + 2
© Carson-Dellosa	© Carson-Dellosa	© Carson-Dellosa

8	9	3
+ 2	+ 2	+ 3

4	5	6
+ 3	+ 3	+ 3

7	8	9
+ 3	+ 3	+ 3

4	5	6
+ 4	+ 4	+ 4
© Carson-Dellosa	© Carson-Dellosa	© Carson-Dellosa

7	8	9
+ 4	+ 4	+ 4
© Carson-Dellosa	© Carson-Dellosa	© Carson-Dellosa

5	6	7
+ 5	+ 5	+ 5
© Carson-Dellosa	© Carson-Dellosa	© Carson-Dellosa

$$\begin{array}{r} 8 \\ + 5 \\ \hline \end{array}$$

$$\begin{array}{r} 9 \\ + 5 \\ \hline \end{array}$$

$$\begin{array}{r} 6 \\ + 6 \\ \hline \end{array}$$

$$\begin{array}{r} 7 \\ + 6 \\ \hline \end{array}$$

$$\begin{array}{r} 8 \\ + 6 \\ \hline \end{array}$$

$$\begin{array}{r} 9 \\ + 6 \\ \hline \end{array}$$

$$\begin{array}{r} 7 \\ + 7 \\ \hline \end{array}$$

$$\begin{array}{r} 8 \\ + 7 \\ \hline \end{array}$$

$$\begin{array}{r} 9 \\ + 7 \\ \hline \end{array}$$

8
+ 8

© Carson-Dellosa

9
+ 8

© Carson-Dellosa

9
+ 9

© Carson-Dellosa

9
− 9

© Carson-Dellosa

9
− 8

© Carson-Dellosa

9
− 7

© Carson-Dellosa

9
− 6

© Carson-Dellosa

9
− 5

© Carson-Dellosa

9
− 4

© Carson-Dellosa

9 − 3	9 − 2	9 − 1
8 − 8	8 − 7	8 − 6
8 − 5	8 − 4	8 − 3

8 − 2	8 − 1	7 − 7
© Carson-Dellosa	© Carson-Dellosa	© Carson-Dellosa
7 − 6	7 − 5	7 − 4
© Carson-Dellosa	© Carson-Dellosa	© Carson-Dellosa
7 − 3	7 − 2	7 − 1
© Carson-Dellosa	© Carson-Dellosa	© Carson-Dellosa

6 − 6	6 − 5	6 − 4
© Carson-Dellosa	© Carson-Dellosa	© Carson-Dellosa
6 − 3	6 − 2	6 − 1
© Carson-Dellosa	© Carson-Dellosa	© Carson-Dellosa
5 − 5	5 − 4	5 − 3
© Carson-Dellosa	© Carson-Dellosa	© Carson-Dellosa

5 − 2	5 − 1	4 − 4
4 − 3	4 − 2	4 − 1
3 − 3	3 − 2	3 − 1

$$\begin{array}{r} 2 \\ -\ 2 \\ \hline \end{array}$$

$$\begin{array}{r} 2 \\ -\ 1 \\ \hline \end{array}$$

$$\begin{array}{r} 1 \\ -\ 1 \\ \hline \end{array}$$